Integrating
Acquired Companies

A volume in the

PROFESSIONAL MANAGEMENT ACCOUNTING SERIES
Edited by JAMES BULLOCH *and* DONALD E. KELLER

INTEGRATING ACQUIRED COMPANIES
Edited by Clark H. Johnson

INTEGRATING ACQUIRED COMPANIES

Management Accounting and Reporting Issues

CLARK H. JOHNSON

Contributors

Tarun K. Bhatia
James Billups
David C. Boehm
William J. Delayo
Joseph L. Fischer
Paul H. Saake
Stanley Stern

A volume in the Professional Management Accounting Series
edited by James Bulloch and Donald E. Keller

A Ronald Press Publication

JOHN WILEY & SONS

New York · Chichester · Brisbane · Toronto · Singapore

This publication is designed to provide accurate and
authoritative information in regard to the subject
matter covered. It is sold with the understanding that
the publisher is not engaged in rendering legal, accounting,
or other professional service. If legal advice or other
expert assistance is required, the services of a competent
professional person should be sought. *From a Declaration
of Principles jointly adopted by a Committee of the
American Bar Association and a Committee of Publishers.*

Library of Congress Cataloging in Publication Data:
Main entry under title:
Integrating acquired companies.

   "A Ronald Press publication."
   Includes index.
   1. Consolidation and merger of corporations—
Accounting—Addresses, essays, lectures. 2. Managerial
accounting—Addresses, essays, lectures. I. Johnson,
Clark H.

HF5686.C7I54   1985   658.1′6   84-23698
ISBN 0-471-80960-8

Printed in the United States of America

10 9 8 7 6 5 4 3 2 1

With love to our wives and children,

Marie, Kevin, David, and Todd Johnson
Barbara, Suzanne, Christine, Jennifer, and Paul Saake
Nancy, Bill, Jr., and Donna Delayo
Jean, Jason, and Janine Billups
Sandi Boehm
Anju Bhatia
Suzanne, Joseph, Keith, and Scott Fischer
Esther, Sara, and Jeffry Stern

PREFACE

This book provides the practical experience and personal opinions of the authors and contributors, and does not represent endorsement by our employer, Johnson & Johnson. A family of 160 companies manufacturing in 50 countries and marketing products in virtually every country, Johnson & Johnson is the largest health care company in the world. Much of our growth over the years has come from acquisitions.

Our former leader, General Robert Wood Johnson, had this to say back in 1967:

Our Track Record in New and Acquired Enterprise

We underrate the capital required
We underestimate the cost of producing the products
We underestimate the strength of competition
We underestimate the technological problems
We underestimate the requirements of management
We underestimate the time required to bring the recently acquired business into a going, successful, profitable and viable establishment
We overestimate the productive capacity of the equipment
We overestimate the quality of a proposed product
We overestimate the potential market
We overestimate the competence of our management

Hopefully, we've made some improvements since 1967, with sales and earnings increasing at annual growth rates of 14% and 16% respectively over the last 16 years, much of it in new and acquired enterprise; but we still recommend keeping "Our Track Record" in clear view.

Even at a return on investment of 20%, *it takes five good investments to pay for one bad one.*

CLARK H. JOHNSON

New Brunswick, New Jersey
January 1985

Special appreciation is extended to the many fellow employees whose encouragement and competent assistance made this book possible. Special recognition goes to Rhonda Valentine-Mitchell, office automation analyst, who expertly processed the manuscript the "new way."

CONTENTS

CONTRIBUTORS

TARUN K. BHATIA is an International Finance Manager with Johnson & Johnson International. He is a Silver Medalist of the CMA examination and is also a CPA. He earned his MBA at Cornell University and was formerly associated with Price Waterhouse & Co.

JAMES BILLUPS is an Internal Audit Supervisor for Johnson & Johnson with previous operating company experience at Personal Products Co. and J&J Dental Products Co. Educated at Rider College, he achieved certification as a CMA.

DAVID C. BOEHM is Director, Finance, of the Instruments Division of Ortho Diagnostic Systems, Inc. He earned his MBA from Rider College and is both a CMA and a CPA.

JAMES BULLOCH is the Managing Director of the Institute of Management Accounting of the National Association of Accountants. Previous to this he served as Professor of Accounting at the University of Michigan. He earned his PhD from the Ohio State University and holds a CPA and a CMA.

WILLIAM J. DELAYO is an Assistant Corporate Controller of Johnson & Johnson who earned his MBA at Rider College. After service as a Captain in the U.S. Marine Corps, he achieved positions as Operations Controller and Marketing Controller at Personal Products Company.

JOSEPH L. FISCHER is Managing Director of Johnson & Johnson A.B. in Stockholm, Sweden. Educated at Penn State University, he served as a Technical Associate of the Financial Accounting Standards Board prior to joining Johnson & Johnson and is a CPA.

CLARK H. JOHNSON is Corporate Controller of Johnson & Johnson. He is a CMA, has a BS in accounting from Rutgers University and an MBA from Fairleigh Dickinson University. Mr. Johnson has worked with Johnson & Johnson since 1953.

DONALD E. KELLER is Chairman of Accounting at Seton Hall University. He is a CMA and CPA and holds a DBA from the University of Southern California. He served as Director of Technical Services for the National Association of Accountants.

PAUL H. SAAKE is Controller of Ortho Diagnostic Systems Inc. and has had diversified experience in both financial and operations accounting. He earned his MBA in Quantitative Analysis at Seton Hall University and became a CPA while employed with Coopers & Lybrand.

STANLEY STERN is Director, Domestic Taxation for Johnson & Johnson. He is a CPA and earned his MBA at New York University. Previous employment included Merck & Co. and Arthur Andersen & Co.

Integrating
Acquired Companies

one

AN OVERVIEW TO INTEGRATING ACQUISITIONS

Clark H. Johnson, MBA, CMA

CONTENTS

INTRODUCTION

Corporate mergers and acquisitions are booming again, reaching toward the heights of the early 1960s and 1970s. Although large deals are highly publicized and their significance has been increasing, the vast majority of transactions are small businesses, many closely held. It is also the case recently that many result from divestitures—but for every seller there is a buyer, so the acquisition process goes on. Investing in acquisitions is risky, but businesses can grow quickly in this way; so acquisitions will likely continue to be a significant part of corporate strategy.

Much has been written about how to value acquisition candidates and other preacquisition activities. However, little has been written about integrating an acquisition into an existing business.

The objective of this book is to provide management with a broad perspective of the many management accounting and reporting considerations involved when integrating an acquisition into a business. Many marriages between companies fail and result in subsequent divestitures. Some of these failures may be attributed to a poor choice of partners; others may be attributed to the way in which acquired businesses are managed after being merged.

THE PARENT–SUBSIDIARY CONFLICT

Small growth companies benefit from a flexible approach to marketing products or services that is the essence of an entrepreneurial environment; however, this flexible approach can be restrained by the usually more structured systems of a large parent. On the other hand, among the reasons why an acquiree is available for acquisition is often weaknesses of the former management, so perhaps they should not be allowed to continue their past methods entirely independently.

Therein lies the conflict in the parent–subsidiary relationship. Most corporations describe themselves as "decentralized," which should mean that managements of their subsidiaries are allowed to operate in an autonomous manner, being evaluated on their end results. A decentralized organizational structure should result in faster and more appropriate decisions in the subsidiaries' marketplace and should result in higher levels of productivity and efficiency with an environment that motivates initiative and creativity.

Needs for Uniformity and Consistency

However, conflicts arise when considering the needs of the parent organization, such as:

Need for a centralized review of plans and investments in order to maximize returns.

Need for cash and debt planning in the most effective manner for the entire enterprise.

Need for consolidated financial statements that are uniform and consistent.

Need for responding to government regulations on matters involving employees, environmental controls, safety, and other matters.

Need for developing managers and assuring that each operating unit has adequate succession plans.

Need for assuring that all subsidiaries operate in the spirit of the parent's ethical standards.

All of these needs and others conflict with the philosophy of decentralization in its purest form and require numerous decisions as to what actions can be effectively decentralized versus those that require centralized procedures.

These choices are readily evident with respect to financial policies, external public reporting, and reporting to top corporate management, all of which tend toward centralization in order to provide uniformity and consistency. However, they can also be achieved in a decentralized organizational structure. Standardization does not necessarily mean centralization.

Centralization Versus Decentralization

Conceptualizing the decentralized environment as compared to the more traditional centralized one can be significant to the manner in which an acquisition is integrated into an existing organization.

Decentralization is fast becoming conventional wisdom in corporate America, but there does not seem to be a singular set of criteria against which to measure whether or not an organization is truly decentralized. Rather, it seems, that organizations develop their own unique structures and cultures.

Recently increased interest in decentralization is probably closely tied to a number of success stories. High-growth companies are more often midsized ($25 million to $1 billion in revenues) or else larger ones that operate in a decentralized manner. Perhaps the basic nature of a decentralized organization is best described as one where each operating unit has its own president and management board. In this structure the parent company's role is primarily financial—making investments, providing capital to the operating units, and evaluating their results.

The latter is where the dots in dotted lines may get closer together when there is a problem. In order to be successful, the decentralized organization depends heavily on selection of the right operating managers rather than getting involved in day-to-day activities. Operating decisions should be made by the operating managers closest to the constituency being served—the customers and their needs. For mid-sized companies these may be relatively small markets. Decentralized units can be more competitive in creating and developing specialized businesses that have clear direction and successfully identify and satisfy customer needs.

Foreign Subsidiaries

The choices in organizational structure and operation are more vivid if one considers an acquisition in another country. Such a subsidiary will be subject to the laws of the country in which it operates and, depending on the country, may be subject to government controls far beyond those in the United States. Local demands may include partial ownership, limitations on repatriations of earnings, requirements that certain raw materials or parts be purchased locally, export requirements, price controls, and many others.

In many cases local customs and per capita income may indicate a need to custom-design products to satisfy local markets. In this kind of an environment, it is easier to understand the need for the subsidiary's managing director to be more of an entrepreneur with considerable independence in order to deal with governmental, labor, and other external relations. Management by local nationals is clearly desirable in this environment.

The parent company operates more like a banker in dealing with a foreign subsidiary in this type of situation. Indeed, that's a good way to identify the basic nature of decentralized management. The parent does have other responsibilities and opportunities, however, such as providing new product technology from sister companies, selection and motivation of key management personnel, and responding to the laws of the parent's home country. For a U.S. parent this includes consolidated financial reporting using U.S. generally accepted accounting principles (GAAP). It also entails very complex reporting to the U.S. Internal Revenue Service with regard to foreign source income—virtually restating earnings of foreign subsidiaries based on U.S. tax regulations. And it also means complying with U.S. legislation such as the Foreign Corrupt Practices Act and reporting of Arab boycotting activities.

So there are many forces that pull in opposite directions in the relationship between an acquired company and headquarters of the parent. Centralization is most often viewed as contributing to profitability through economy of size; with it comes increased bureaucracy and red tape. Decentralization is seen to provide opportunities for innovation in adapting to market opportunities and local environments; a level of flexibility and freedom that motivates creativity and productivity.

Regardless of the structure inherent in an organization, the requirements for unified and consistent financial reporting exist and must be woven into the structural fabric.

TYPES OF ACQUISITIONS

The nature of an acquisition is also a major consideration in how it will be integrated into the existing business. Vertical mergers are more likely to be integrated in a centralized fashion, while conglomerate acquisitions are more likely to be integrated in a decentralized way. In between are many other types of acquisitions, such as those with primary purposes of bringing new technology or new markets to the existing business.

There are a variety of reasons why business combinations occur. Some result from a strategic planning process that has identified specific objectives. For example, these could be objectives for growth requiring new products or technology or specific needs for strengthening certain functions such as manufacturing or distribution. In other situations acquisitions may result from seizing opportunities without a specific fit with the present business. This wide range in types of acquisitions can result in a similarly wide variety of ways in which they are integrated into the present business. One way of classifying types of acquisitions is by broadly classifying them as conglomerate, vertical, or horizontal.

Conglomerate Acquisitions

Conglomerate acquisitions have become less fashionable since many of those in the sixties have been unsuccessful and led to later divestment.

A conglomerate merger is when a company with dissimilar products or technology is acquired. These acquisitions usually have a financial reason, such as improving profitability or plans to sell off the assets after acquisition. These acquisitions usually occur when market values are depressed below the underlying value of the assets or when a business has liquidity or cash problems.

Conglomerate acquisitions are the candidates most likely to be kept free-standing and managed in a decentralized fashion by their new parent.

Vertical Acquisitions

Vertical acquisitions are those most likely to be integrated into present operations. The purpose of vertical integration is to deliver current products more effectively by controlling the sources of raw materials or manufacture; or, for a manufacturer, it means acquiring the marketing and distribution systems and delivering finished products to ultimate consumers.

Vertical combinations are more likely to be integrated in a centralized fashion often with the acquiree's former business no longer identifiable. Even in a decentralized corporation, a vertical acquisition for or by an existing subsidiary is likely to lose its identity or become a second-tier subsidiary that will be managed in a centralized fashion by the acquiring subsidiary.

Horizontal Acquisitions

These arise when both companies are selling products in the same market. There may be an overlap in product lines, but the combined line is generally wider. There may be common customers, with the new market containing a broader customer base.

Horizontal integration has the potential benefit of developing synergy in growth and market share—synergy is when one plus one equals three. In some cases it is similar technology that is being merged, in which case synergy may occur by creating new ideas. Since the research and technical side of most businesses is deeply immersed in developing and protecting existing products, new ideas often have to come from outside of the existing business.

Whereas conglomerates are more likely to be managed in a decentralized manner, and vertical acquisitions are more likely to lose their identity or be managed in a centralized fashion, horizontal mergers may be integrated in either manner depending on the circumstances and the prevailing management culture.

INTEGRATION PROCESSES

The process of integration starts long before the legal transfer of ownership— the human element has its roots in the very first contact between representatives of the two companies. As the investigation turns into negotiation, human factors become an important determinant in making a fair deal.

In addition to having built the present business into one of interest to the acquiror, the owners or key managers may have a key role to play in achieving the future success anticipated by the acquiror. It is important to deal with the acquiree fairly and honestly so that they will have favorable attitudes toward their new parent company and continue their role in the new business with enthusiasm (although sometimes it is difficult to motivate a millionaire).

It is desirable to explain that at some point in time there may be some changes. Since almost all acquisitions are at a premium over market value, higher returns of the combined businesses must be expected—meaning changes. Furthermore, the management styles of both businesses are likely to be different—meaning changes.

The Human Element

The human element should automatically be considered a probable problem highest on the list of priorities in the integration process.

Those involved in the negotiation are likely to be highly supportive of the merger to a fault—not seeing potential problems. Others, who have not participated in the negotiation process, likely will not share this enthusiasm. Their unanswered questions and concerns will create feelings of insecurity, which may be expressed as defensiveness and open opposition to changes after the merger. And changes will be inevitable.

Clearly, these problems could be minimized or even avoided with adequate planning and communications. The focus should be on how the new subsidiary will operate, what will be expected by the new parent, what the new parent will provide (beyond cash, this might include technology or other resources of new sister businesses), policies and practices of the parent (particularly compensation and benefits), and generally, in what ways the new merger will benefit both the parent and subsidiary. Unfortunately, all of this takes time, and time is often of the essence in the acquisition process.

While not always practical prior to the merger, though, this planning and communications should be highest on the list of priorities during the integration process in order to reassure and enlist the support of employees whose continued contributions are needed. Furthermore, it should be recognized that not all of the changes will occur at the new subsidiary—there may be some changes, albeit to a lesser extent, to the parent—particularly if the acquiree is relatively large (i.e., more than 20% of the parent's size).

Accomplishing the planning and communications requires talented management staff of both parties who can be made available for these tasks. The very concept of planning is to provide coordination and control, which are essential elements in the integration process.

Full integration takes time. It is foolhardy to think that a parent's management team can march in like conquering heroes and introduce changes quickly in the face of significant resistance.

However, the acquiring management must have adequate financial and management controls, regardless of whether the newly acquired business is to be managed in a centralized or decentralized mode. This usually means that initial control is best achieved by learning and using the acquiree's existing systems. Then changes can be introduced in a rational manner with less resistance. Simply imposing new ways quickly brings back memories of the "Theory X" style of management that assumes all employees are lazy and reinforces "we and they" attitudes.

The orientation of accountants to uniformity of information and systems means that they may be the most likely to create behavioral problems by insisting upon immediate conformance to the parent's financial planning cycles, accounting methods, and internal management reporting systems. Surely all of these need to be addressed in due course, but with proper attention to effective ways of introducing changes.

Evaluation of Subsidiary Finance Staff

Most acquired companies are small businesses and many of them were not publicly traded. The result of becoming part of a large, publicly traded company can be a tremendous shock and the external reporting requirements an onerous burden, especially if it is intended that the new subsidiary will continue to operate somewhat autonomously, such as in a conglomerate or highly decentralized organization.

Indeed, the new subsidiary may not have a finance staff with adequate training or experience to deal with the new accounting and reporting burdens. The parent will have to recognize this problem early and provide adequate resources. Assistance from corporate staff may be the best temporary arrangement, until staffing needs can be clearly identified and satisfied.

In another scenario the acquired company may have been more sophisticated with a CFO who had responsibilities for public reporting and financing of the business. As a result of the acquisition, these important functions will likely be provided by the parent and the subsidiaries' key financial person will be primarily responsible for controllership functions. This may result in the need for a change of personnel in the best interests of the persons involved, as well as the business. Hasty changes, however, are not desirable. The new parent can learn a great deal about the business from the acquiree's CFO and may indeed identify another position for him or her in the corporate organization. For this individual, the new parent may provide broader career opportunities than previously imagined. Patience and mutual respect during the learning and integrating stages will generally result in mutual benefits.

MANAGEMENT ACCOUNTING ISSUES

Accounting for the acquisition also has its roots in the preacquisition investigation and negotiation stages. It was during that process that prior financial statements should have been acquired and evaluated. A preacquisition audit should have identified the accounting practices of the acquiree and how they differed from the parent. An acquisition audit at the closing date should have determined not only the final purchase price but also what adjustments will be needed to consolidate the acquiree. And the acquisition planning should have determined the tax consequences of the transaction and the accounting method to be used—pooling or purchase.

With all due concern as to how to effectively introduce changes to the new subsidiary, the new parent has assumed many responsibilities at the time of the closing. The new subsidiary has to be consolidated in any publicly reported financial statements—whether the transaction occurred almost three months ago or barely several days before the end of the accounting period. A preacquisition audit may not have been done. Audited financial statements of the acquiree may not have been available. An acquisition audit may not have been finished. Or, the transaction may have been so confidential that finance staff was inadequately involved in the acquisition process. So problems may spring eternal for the corporate finance staff!

Sections of this book address a number of these issues which straddle the planning and integrating phases—before and after the closing date. Even if not planned, they still have to be implemented.

Management Responsibilities

Regardless of whether an acquisition will be integrated in a centralized or decentralized manner, certain management accounting and reporting issues will need to be addressed.

1. Internal financial controls and how the parent will be assured that these are adequate on a continuing basis.
2. Financial policies and procedures, including what activities and expenditures require preapproval by the parent.
3. Accounting changes needed in order to provide uniformity of consolidated financial statements may include restatements of historical information.
4. Management reporting to the parent—content, timing, format—for both actual results and planning cycles.

In a centralized environment issues will go deeper; for example, converting to the parent's billing or payroll systems or having all accounting services provided by the parent.

Assurance of Internal Financial Controls

In a centralized environment the acquired company will generally lose its identity and the parent's system of internal financial controls will prevail. However, in a decentralized organizational structure, this issue requires more attention; but internal financial control can be exercised with systems such as:

1. Written corporate policies and financial procedures.
2. Internal auditing with written reports to line corporate management and required operating unit responses and follow-up.
3. External (public) audits with similar reporting/responses.
4. Financial plans, regular reporting against plans, and management review of variances.
5. Control of cash and approval of all borrowings by the parent.
6. Approval by the parent of capital investments and employee compensation above certain monetary levels.
7. Certification signed by subsidiary management regarding compliance with governmental regulations and the parent's ethical standards.
8. Organizational reviews and on-site visits by corporate officials.

Control the Cash!

Acquired companies are usually not as well off as expected, particularly those with solvency problems. Despite preacquisition investigations and audits, one of the early steps in the integration process for financial management of both the parent company and subsidiary is to reassess current financing problems so that they can be addressed promptly. Besides, the basic way to control a business is to control the cash, whether management is centralized or decentralized (more important in the latter case).

Many companies are available for acquisition because of a lack of capital. A successful business may be growing faster than it can provide needed working capital and expansion of capacity. On the other hand, an acquisition that is in a loss position has deeper problems.

Inadequate cash flow results in management spending a lot of time dealing with creditors, trying to obtain supplies, and juggling available funds in order to keep the business afloat. The new parent should assume responsibility for the cash situation, thereby providing funds needed or making arrangements for borrowings. This action will free subsidiary management to turn its full attention toward operations and improving profitability.

Available funds should be consolidated with the parent's portfolio in order to maximize investment opportunities. Borrowings should be managed by the parent in order to maximize leverage. Where these cash management techniques are not practical, perhaps with a foreign subsidiary for example, the parent may want to retain the authority to approve lines of credit needed by the subsidiary during the future planning period and/or establish a policy on acceptable investments of available cash.

Special International Considerations

Acquisition of a foreign company heightens the awareness to differences and the problems of integration. First one learns that who is the foreigner depends only on where one's home is. We are all foreigners when away from home, and many people resent the label. A lesson in sensitivity is so important in working with people in different social, political, and economic environments.

As discussed in Chapter 6, there are many special considerations when integrating an international acquisition, a number of which revolve around regulatory requirements already imposed by the local country on the subsidiary, which now must also be concerned with the laws of the parent's country and also its GAAP.

The language barrier may prove more demanding than expected. Even in accounting, terms are different and written explanations easily misunderstood.

External Reporting

The two methods of accounting for business combinations—purchase or pooling of interests—are described in Chapter 7. Also covered are the consolidation process, including translation of foreign currency financial statements, as well as several matters of external reporting that smaller acquirees probably have not had to disclose—Segments of Business, Changing Prices and Lease Commitments.

Essentially, a pooling of interests is accomplished with an exchange of shares of stock; the new combination is accounted-for as though it always existed. Therefore, upon acquisition, financial results are consolidated retrospectively with restatement of prior periods, unless immaterial. This may be a burdensome work requirement for both the parent and subsidiary. On the other hand, purchase accounting is similar to purchase of any asset; sales and earnings are consolidated prospectively only from the date of closing.

The pros and cons of purchase versus pooling accounting revolve around the matters of goodwill amortization, the tax basis of assets acquired, dilution of earnings per share, and liquidity in cash versus stock and taxable versus nontaxable considerations for the seller. Financial modeling techniques are very useful in analyzing the myriad possibilities when choosing between these methods with their financing and profitability implications.

Pooling treatment requirements are very specific under APB 16 and require careful planning and execution; all other transactions are of the purchase variety.

With respect to consolidation of a foreign acquisition, the translation rules are complex. However, even more significant to the new subsidiary will be the requirement to report results consistent with U.S. GAAP. In many countries this will require a number of adjusting entries from their local statutory and tax reporting accounts. Knowledge of U.S. GAAP and proficiency with the English language by a local national commands a high salary and attracts only a limited slate of candidates for financial directors in many countries.

Tax Matters

Tax issues, as explained more thoroughly in Chapter 8, cover a broad variety of considerations.

Initial tax planning concerns itself with how to arrange a tax-free reorganization versus a taxable acquisition of either stock or assets. Buyer and seller often have conflicting interests in this regard, so potential adverse tax costs may be a significant item during negotiations. Competent appraisal of assets may be important to future profitability as well as defending against IRS challenges.

Once acquired, the new subsidiary may continue as a separate legal entity or become part of the parent or one of its subsidiaries. Tax expense for the controlled group could be considerably different depending on the form in which the new business is operated.

There may also be marketing considerations in this regard. Since brand names and trademarks are often contained in company names, and packages of consumer products must identify the legal entity, marketing advantages may outweigh tax considerations. Although the U.S. government allows consolidation of federal tax returns, most states do not. Furthermore, many states do not allow carry-over of losses. Hence planning, and anticipating the unplanned, take on increased importance.

Certain accounting methods require election for tax purposes. If the acquired company is structured as a division of the new parent, those accounting methods elected by the parent generally apply to the new acquiree. Careful planning is also needed if the requirements for utilizing a net operating loss carry-over are to be met.

Consolidated federal tax returns are usually desirable, but this requires the same fiscal years for tax purposes and may mean changing that of the acquiree, a short tax year, and extra work.

All of these tax matters need to be considered by the parent's corporate tax staff with thorough knowledge of the entire business, whether the acquiree is managed in either a decentralized or centralized manner. Once again, consolidated financial planning and reporting may seem to be in conflict with a decentralized management style but can be achieved with cooperative efforts in the best interests of the corporation. Providing recognition and "credit" to the participants are important motivators in assuring co-operation.

CONCLUSION

The integration of acquisitions needs talented management capable of introducing changes effectively. It's an exciting and challenging process; ineptness could mean failure of the marriage. Even at a return on investment of 20%, *it takes five good investments to pay for one bad one.*

CHECKLIST

1. *Management Culture*
   (a) Centralized versus decentralized organization structure
   (b) Special considerations of international acquisitions
2. *Needs for Uniformity and Consistency*
   (a) Centralized review of plans and investments
   (b) Cash and debt planning
   (c) Consolidated financial statements
   (d) Responding to government regulations
   (e) Developing managers
   (f) Ethical standards

3. *Types of Acquisitions*
   (a) Vertical
   (b) Conglomerate
   (c) Horizontal
4. *Integration Processes*
   (a) Human elements
   (b) Management staff time
   (c) Methods of introducing changes
   (d) Evaluation of CFO and staff of acquiree
5. *Management Accounting Issues*
   (a) Preacquisition audit
   (b) Acquisition audit
   (c) Tax consequences and planning
   (d) Consolidation requirements
   (e) Pooling versus purchase
   (f) Internal financial controls
   (g) Financial policies and procedures
   (h) Accounting alternatives
   (i) Management reporting
   (j) Planning cycles
   (k) Control the cash!
   (l) Compliance certifications
   (m) U.S. GAAP
   (n) External reporting

two

A CENTRALIZED APPROACH

Paul H. Saake, MBA, CPA

CONTENTS

THE PURPOSE OF THE CENTRALIZED APPROACH

Purpose

This chapter outlines the practical approach to implementing a centralized organizational philosophy and financial reporting system. Only acquisitions between two U.S. companies will be addressed, however, this approach can be utilized when a U.S. company acquires a foreign business entity as well.

In order to present the total picture, a summary will be made that compares and contrasts the policies and procedures, management structure, reporting requirements, and other operating criteria relevant to a centralized versus a decentralized management philosophy. Ultimately, the centralized approach, which many U.S. companies have adopted, will be detailed using the working example of folding a new subsidiary into the current organizational and financial structure of the parent company.

Defining the Approaches

Business combinations, mergers, and acquisitions take many different forms and are entered into for various reasons. Successful companies are continually searching for new business opportunities that will provide profit improvement through one or more of the following means:

1. New technology associated with the company's existing product line.
2. New markets for existing technology or product lines.
3. Diversification into completely new technology and new markets.

Over the past several years, a significant number of acquisitions have occurred as a result of major companies diversifying into new technology and new markets to improve their potential long-term growth. During the acquisition process, the answer to the following question must have been addressed by management: "How is the new subsidiary or division going to be integrated into our organizational and financial structure?" The discussion generated will lead to the following query: "Is the centralized or decentralized approach going to be established with respect to the new subsidiary?" Depending on the current circumstances, the answers to the above questions can be very easy or difficult to formulate. If the companies prior to the acquisition had a customer–supplier relationship, the centralized approach may be selected for the merger; a diversification into a new industry will most likely utilize the decentralized approach. The financial reporting requirements of a subsidiary are the results of the management philosophy (centralized versus decentralized) implemented by the surviving company. Accounting for the acquisition as a pooling of interests or a purchase has no impact on this decision.

From this point on the acquiring company will be referred to as the corporation and the acquired company as the subsidiary.

The *decentralized approach* to management and financial reporting does not have a significant impact upon the new subsidiary. The subsidiary's management team and business objectives remain intact. External financial reporting is replaced by financial requirements established by the finance division of the corporation for consolidation purposes. The new subsidiary may need to make some changes in its internal financial reporting structure to meet the requirements of the corporation and its policies and procedures.

The *centralized approach* to management and financial reporting has a significant impact upon the new subsidiary. The subsidiary's identity as a separate organization is dissolved because it inherits the name of the surviving corporation, and various functions (selling, marketing, finance, personnel) are consolidated. External financial reporting ceases at the date of the acquisition and internal financial reporting requirements are significantly changed as the subsidiary becomes integrated into the corporation's management philosophy and financial policies and procedures.

Centralized Versus Decentralized

The major differences between the centralized approach and the decentralized approach are summarized as follows:

Centralized Approach	Decentralized Approach
1. The subsidiary's identity as a separate organization is dissolved.	1. Subsidiary maintains identity.
2. The subsidiary's management structure and responsibilities change as the company is being integrated.	2. The subsidiary's management structure and responsibilities remain intact.

Centralized Approach	Decentralized Approach
3. The subsidiary's financial policies and procedures change significantly in order to be integrated with the corporation's financial systems.	3. The subsidiary's financial policies and procedures are adapted to the corporation's policies and procedures. Internal financial reporting remains intact.
4. Operational efficiencies are gained by the consolidation of various functions.	4. No significant operational efficiencies are implemented as a result of the merger.
5. As the intergration occurs, new methods to evaluate the financial performance of the subsidiary must be developed.	5. The subsidiary's financial performance continues to be measured as a separate company.
6. The mission and strategy of the subsidiary continues to be altered during the integration period.	6. The mission and strategy of the subsidiary are not significantly altered.
7. The businesses short- and long-range strategies are developed at the corporate office with input from the subsidiary's management.	7. The businesses short- and long-range strategies are developed at the subsidiary and approved by the corporate office.
8. Increased marketing potential because the subsidiary is now identified with the surviving corporation.	8. The association of the two companies does not enhance the marketing potential.
9. Subsidiary benefits by the expertise in the areas of manufacturing, marketing, and administration of the corporation as well as from being able to tap the corporation's resources for funding future projects.	9. Areas of expertise are often in unrelated industries so benefits are not significant except for the availability of capital for future projects.

The management philosophy, centralized versus decentralized, has a significant impact on the subsidiary's financial policies and procedures as well as the operating philosophy of the new subsidiary. This is a key decision that must be discussed and made by the acquiring corporation prior to performing the preacquisition financial evaluation and analyses. The implementation of the centralized approach will take up to two years to complete but depends on the size and the complexity of the company being acquired. A detailed integration plan must be developed and implemented by both the corporation and the new subsidiary's management team.

INTEGRATION PROCESS

Management's Approach

The centralized approach to integrating a subsidiary can be implemented on the date of the acquisition or it can be phased in over the course of several years. Implementation is primarily based on management's operating philosophy and commitment as well as the complexity and the size of the company being acquired. A successful integration program on the date of the acquisition of the new subsidiary is one that implements the corporation's sales order processing, finished goods inventory, accounts receivable, accounts payable, payroll, and general ledger systems with communication capabilities through computer facilities. This requires a considerable amount of preplanning, coordination, and communication between the two companies. If management is unable to decide during preacquisition discussions on how to manage the newly acquired subsidiary (separate company versus a division), the total integration process could take over two years to complete because of lack of direction and planning. A situation like this can be frustrating to the corporation's and subsidiary's management staffs because organization and financial responsibilities would be in continuous transition.

Timing of Discussions

Prior to the acquisition, the financial management of both companies should meet, preferably at the suitor company's headquarters, to discuss the financial, administrative, and operational issues that will have an impact upon both companies and to develop a program to resolve any differences. This meeting should be scheduled as early as possible during the acquisition negotiations so that an integration program can be timely developed and implemented. Among the operational issues that must be addressed as soon as possible are the computer capabilities of the new subsidiary because new computer equipment lead times can be lengthy. Also, program changes to current corporate systems to handle a new location, current financial policies and procedures, and adequate training of personnel require adequate time and human resources for implementation. During this meeting, an implementation program outlining the responsibilities of each company's financial management leading to the integration of the financial systems policies and procedures must be developed, as well as establishing a communication system to follow up on the progress of the program.

The subsidiary's financial management should have an opportunity to meet with the key financial managers of the corporation to discuss in more detail the financial policies and procedures as well as any potential problem areas. This type of communication will assist each participant to become more familiar with the financial organization structure along with the financial capabilities and requirements of each company. A copy of all financial and accounting policies and procedures manuals should be provided to the subsidiary's management for its review and evaluation. This will enable the subsidiary's financial management to implement changes to its current policies and procedures prior to the acquisition and to assist in identifying potential problems that will have to be resolved prior to the systems integration.

A visit to another subsidiary of the corporation by the new subsidiary's financial management might be advisable. This will give them the opportunity to discuss the centralized approach and the integration program with a management team that has experienced this type of transition. Specific questions concerning the organization structure, financial policies and procedures, interface with the corporate office, and routine activities can be addressed. This gives the new management the opportunity to observe an operating unit which reflects the organizational philosophy and structure it is currently responsible for implementing.

Key Financial Areas To Be Addressed

The key areas that must be addressed during the integration process are as follows:

1. *Systems Integration*
    (a) Which financial systems will be integrated with the corporate systems?
    (b) When will the systems be implemented?
    (c) What new computer equipment is required to implement the program?
    (d) When will the training take place?

(e) Will the corporate systems have to be upgraded/changed to handle the additional activity?

2. *Financial Requirements*

(a) What financial data will be required by the corporation on the date of the acquisition, as well as weekly, monthly, quarterly, and annually after the acquisition?

(b) What historical data must be developed and be available?

(c) When and how will a financial forecast be developed?

3. *Financial Policies and Procedures*

(a) Which policies and procedures must be implemented immediately (lock box, sales reporting, etc.)?

(b) When will the remaining policies and procedures be implemented (accounts receivable, accounts payable, payroll, etc.)?

(c) When will financial reporting requirements be implemented?

4. *Transfer of Responsibilities*

(a) When will the transfer of responsibilities take place?

(b) Are there overlapping responsibilities (i.e., accounts receivable prior to the acquisition collected by the subsidiary while the corporate office collects all receivables after the acquisition)?

(c) Who is responsible for implementing the program?

5. *Organizational Changes*

(a) Does the new organization structure support the centralized approach?

(b) When will the new organization be implemented?

6. *Responsibility Reporting*

(a) What internal financial reports must be developed to support the new organizational responsibilities?

(b) When will the new financial reports be developed to support the centralized approach?

(c) When will the reports be approved and implemented?

Communication to Management

After the integration program to support the centralized approach has been developed, communication between both entities' management is imperative to the success of the program. Bi-weekly meetings to review the status of the program, as well as to address and resolve current problems should be established. If necessary, weekly meetings concerning a key area (implementation of a computer integration program) should be established so that this part of the integration program is properly coordinated within both companies and implemented on time.

ORGANIZATIONAL STRUCTURE

Reporting Relationships

The organization chart shown in Exhibit 2.1 presents the organization structure of the subsidiary and corporate office prior to and after the acquisition. In the centralized approach, the general manager at the subsidiary location has direct responsibility for manufacturing, material management, and the purchasing functions and indirect responsibility for finance, research, and personnel. The marketing function is consolidated with the corporate func-

Exhibit 2.1   Organization Chart

Prior to the Acquisition

Corporate	*Subsidiary*
┌─ President	┌─ President
├─ Vice President of Operations	├─ Director of Manufacturing
├─ Vice President of Finance	├─ Treasurer
├─ Vice President of Personnel	├─ Director of Personnel
├─ Vice President of Research	├─ Vice President of Research
└─ Vice President of Marketing	└─ Vice President of Marketing

After the Acquisition

Corporate	*Subsidiary*
┌─ President	
├─ Vice President of Operations ─────────	General Manager
├─ Vice President of Finance ─────────	Plant Controller
├─ Vice President of Personnel ─────────	Manager of Personnel
├─ Vice President of Research ─────────	Director of Research
└─ Vice President of Marketing	

tion. The finance, research, and personnel functions report to the respective vice presidents at the corporate office.

Commitment of Management

The integration of the organization structure and responsibility take a considerable amount of planning and communication combined with management's total commitment to the centralized approach philosophy. Because subsidiary management's responsibilities will significantly change during this transition period, it is very important that every employee understands the objective of the program. If the program is not communicated properly by top management, then employee frustration and high turnover can be anticipated at the subsidiary during the transition period because of the apprehension and misunderstanding resulting from the changes in job responsibility, scope, and authority. The steps to implement the centralized approach are as follows:

1. Define operating philosophy and strategic plan.
2. Develop organization structure based on the operating philosophy and objectives.
3. Communicate operating philosophy, strategic plan, and organizational structure to line management.
4. Develop financial reporting policies and procedures to meet the requirements of the operating philosophy, strategic plan, and organization structure.
5. Implement financial reporting programs.
6. Monitor operating results of the subsidiary in relation to operating philosophy and strategic plan.

SYSTEMS INTEGRATION

Computerized Systems Evaluation

Systems integration depends on the sophistication of the computerized systems of both companies. One reason why a company would want to be acquired is because its current manual and/or computerized systems cannot properly process the current volume of activity and cannot be upgraded to meet the capacity needed for future growth. Current systems of a small company are normally established to assist in preparation of financial data and routine functions (i.e., payroll, accounts payable, accounts receivable). Data to assist management in operating and analyzing the current business activity is not readily available. Also it is very expensive for a small company to implement state-of-the-art systems to process sales, accounts receivable, inventory planning, fixed assets, accounts payable, and financial reporting. In this situation the subsidiary will benefit from the resources available at corporate that can be immediately integrated and implemented. A successful systems integration program can eliminate a major problem facing the subsidiary prior to the acquisition and enable management to now turn its attention to the future growth of the business with no short-term systems restrictions.

The timing and the mechanism of systems integration must be addressed by operational and data processing management prior to the acquisition to allow ample time to resolve any hardware and software compatibility problems that might arise. The method of transmitting data electronically to and from both locations must be decided upon quickly so that the appropriate hardware and software can be identified and purchased. Defining and implementing this phase of the integration program depends on the complexity of the computer systems and programs involved as well as on the relative sophistication of both companies in the area of data processing.

Financial Systems

The following financial systems are generally integrated when the centralized approach is implemented, resulting in the standardization of financial procedures:

1. General ledger.
2. Accounts payable.
3. Payroll and benefits.
4. Sales order processing.
5. Accounts receivable.
6. Inventory management and control.
7. Fixed assets.
8. Budgeting.

The above systems are not listed in order of importance or timing of implementation. The approach to the systems integration program depends on the objectives and strategic plan of the corporation. The key elements within these financial systems are summarized below:

System	Requirements
General Ledger	Chart of accounts, systems expansion for a new location, summarization structure, budget data, year-to-date balances (pooling of interests), journal entry procedures.
Accounts Payable	Chart of accounts, vendor file, systems expansion for a new location, batch control procedures.
Payroll	Chart of accounts, employee history file, benefits data, year-to-date earnings, year-to-date taxes, withholdings.
Sales Order Processing	Product description, product code, unit of measure, unit pricing table, special handling, freight policy, sales terms, customer listing, sales unit and dollar history.
Accounts Receivable	Customer listing, sales terms, invoice data, payment data, payment history, outstanding balances, invoices at implementation, cash application.
Inventory Management Systems	Raw material, work-in-process and finished-goods codes, standard costs, unit of measure, reorder points, production requirements, product structure, vendor history, vendor performance, data entry procedures.

Documentation and Training

If each system to be integrated is documented by corporate policies and procedures that can be utilized by the subsidiary's management, the systems integration program will proceed very smoothly. Formal training programs must be developed and scheduled for all new users. During the implementation phase, certain key employees (both subsidiary and corporate) must be available to assist in troubleshooting and resolving unforeseen problems that will arise. Planning, communication, and coordination are the keys to an efficient and successful system integration program.

FINANCIAL POLICIES AND PROCEDURES

Timing of Events

The centralized approach requires that the corporate financial policies and procedures be integrated into the new subsidiary's financial systems. Depending on the complexity of the financial area being integrated, certain policies and procedures can be implemented on the day of the acquisition (cash management) while others may require months or years to implement (integrated cost system). A general list of procedures that must be evaluated and will be discussed in this section is as follows:

1. Financial reporting requirements.
2. Financial forecasting requirements.
3. Strategic plan reporting.
4. Property, plant, and equipment
   (a) Capitalization
   (b) Depreciation
5. Inventory accounting and valuation.
6. Intercompany accounting.
7. Investment in the corporate portfolio.
8. Employee cost reporting.
9. Capital appropriation requests.
10. Accounting for special incentive compensation programs.
11. Lease accounting and reporting.
12. Cash management.
13. Expenditure delegation.
14. Payroll systems.

This chapter does not specifically address the policies and procedures concerning accounts receivable, accounts payable, other assets, and other liabilities because these accounts would be consolidated at the corporate office. Also, affiliate transactions will be minimal as a result of the corporate office handling and processing all major expenditures for the subsidiary. All intercompany transactions associated with sales, purchases, receivables, and payables would be eliminated in consolidation in accordance with generally accepted accounting principles. The financial forecasting and reporting requirements are presented later in this chapter.

Cash and Working Capital Management

Control over cash management is automatically transferred to the corporate office. A centralized lock box system should be established immediately for all cash remittances, and the investment of surplus funds becomes the responsibility of the corporate office. Since a centralized cash disbursement system is implemented, cash requirements at the subsidiary will be minimal; an imprest amount to handle routine transactions like cash advances, small expenditures, and miscellaneous transactions (CODs) should be sufficient. The subsidiary's checking account will have a dollar limit per check depending on the size of the operation, and each check should require two signatures. The bank account will function like an imprest account and will be reimbursed when proper documentation is submitted to the corporate office. A petty cash imprest account will also be established at the subsidiary.

Payroll System

Another disbursement system that will be centralized is the payroll system. The corporate office will be responsible for processing the checks and reimbursing the payroll imprest account for each payroll. Often the payroll checks will be drawn on a bank account that is not located in the same state as the subsidiary. In states that require payroll checks be drawn on a bank located within that state, arrangements can be established with a local bank to cash employee payroll checks drawn on an out-of-state bank account for a fee or compensating balance.

Expenditure Delegation and Authorization

An integral part of the process of paying bills and ordering merchandise is the expenditure delegation and authorization procedure. This procedure must be developed, implemented, and documented. The dollar limits for each management position must be in line with the position's responsibility and authority, with consideration of the size of the operation. The expenditure authorization is for the processing of purchase requisitions, purchase orders, check requisitions, invoices, cash advances, and petty cash. This procedure will require that each expenditure authorization be documented in writing, signed by the current incumbent, and approved by the vice president of finance.

Inventory Valuation

Implementing inventory financial policies and procedures is among the most difficult tasks. The difficulties are caused by the inventory valuation requirements for acquisition under generally accepted accounting principles, the subsidiary's normal inventory valuation system (LIFO, FIFO, etc.), the complexity of the cost accounting system, and method of keeping track of inventory quantities.

Generally accepted accounting principles provide that inventory acquired in a business combination accounted for by the purchase method is to be valued according to the following guidelines:

Raw material—current replacement cost.

Work-in-process—net realizable value less a reasonable profit.

Finished goods—net realizable value less a reasonable profit.

Inventories acquired in a business combination accounted for as a pooling of interests are valued at the recorded cost of the acquired entity.

To have one subsidiary valuing inventory using the first-in–first-out (FIFO) method while the last-in–first-out (LIFO) method is used at another subsidiary is not unusual. In this circumstance a corporate procedure must be developed so that the external reporting requirements concerning inventory valuation and disclosure are met. For external reporting requirements the inventory valuation methods must be described along with the income statement impact of the LIFO versus FIFO method, and significant liquidations of the LIFO layer within the period.

An evaluation of the new subsidiary's cost accounting system must be accomplished immediately so that recommendations outlining the necessary changes to make the operation consistent from an inventory valuation perspective can be developed and implemented. This evaluation will entail a detailed review of cost items that are included in standard cost (gross inventory valuation) and cost items that are treated as cost-not-in-standard or period costs. Once inconsistencies are identified, a program to implement the changes can be developed. If a subsidiary is currently determining the inventory value at the close of each accounting period by taking a physical inventory because an inventory tracking and financial reporting system does not exist, the development of a fully integrated standard cost and cost reporting system can become a lengthy process.

The subsidiary's inventories must be analyzed for slow-moving, obsolete, and excess merchandise. This analysis can be completed in conjunction with the first physical inventory. Guidelines regarding slow-moving, obsolete, and excess inventories will have to be developed and implemented in accordance with the corporate procedures. A review of the documentation that supports all inventory reserve accounts must be analyzed by corporate management. Judgment must be exercised when determining whether an inventory write-up or write-down is necessary.

Intercompany Profits

If prior to the acquisition the subsidiary was and continues to be a supplier to the acquiring corporation, then the unrealized intercompany profit in inventory must be eliminated after the acquisition. Either a procedure to eliminate the intercompany profit or a transfer pricing at cost procedure must be developed and implemented. This is a major financial decision because, administratively, it is very difficult to track and eliminate the intercompany profit in inventory at the end of each financial period. The transfer pricing concept impacts upon the profitability of the subsidiary, but has no impact upon the consolidated financial results. However, there are financial approaches to assist management in evaluating the profit contribution of an operating unit. The approaches are presented later in this chapter.

Capitalization and Depreciation

The capitalization and depreciation policies and procedures of the subsidiary must be evaluated. Whether the merger is a pooling of interest or a purchase has an impact upon the fixed-asset balances and depreciation methods. Tax law ramifications must also be evaluated by management. Generally, the following approach would be taken:

> *Pooling of Interests.* The assets are consolidated at current book value, and the depreciation methods used prior to the acquisition will continue to be utilized for those assets that are on the books at the date of the acquisition. All new assets purchased after the acquisition can be depreciated in accordance with the corporate policy (any method meeting the financial and tax reporting requirements can be utilized).
>
> *Purchase.* The appraisal value of the assets is capitalized, and the corporate depreciation policy can be utilized.

A physical inventory and tagging of all fixed assets should be completed as soon as practical after the acquisition. This will not only assist management in identifying and properly utilizing all fixed assets but will serve to establish the necessary data base for a computerized fixed-asset system. To control capital expenditures at the corporate office, a capital appropriation procedure will be developed and implemented. This procedure will specify capital expenditure approval limits and a routing system through which all capital appropriations will have to circulate for final approval.

FINANCIAL FORECASTING AND REPORTING REQUIREMENTS

Centralized Versus Decentralized Approach

As two separate entities, each corporation's performance is evaluated based on profit objectives as well as other financial goals such as predetermined balance sheet ratio targets. After the acquisition, the method of measuring performance depends upon the approach selected by the corporation as follows:

Centralized Approach. New evaluation methods and financial reports must be developed and implemented to measure the operating performance of the subsidiary, especially if major functions, such as marketing, are consolidated after the acquisition.

Decentralized Approach. Current evaluation methods and financial reports will continue with only minimum changes to meet the corporate requirements.

The centralized approach is more difficult to implement because the financial reports and data that were utilized in the past to evaluate the business' performance will not be available. Most operating companies' profitability is measured by the income statement or net income as a percent of sales or investment. Once the centralized organizational and financial structures are in place in conjunction with the consolidation of certain functions, an income statement does not represent the financial performance of the new subsidiary or plant location.

How can the operating performance of the new subsidiary be measured? The development of financial reports to meet corporate and subsidiary managements' objectives requires an in-depth understanding of each facet of the business and the financial reporting systems combined with financial creativity.

In implementing the centralized approach, corporate and subsidiary management must understand the impact this approach will have on the organization structure, operating unit functions, and financial reporting requirements. The management structure with defined responsibilities must be in place prior to developing and implementing a financial reporting system for the subsidiary. The financial data to be submitted monthly, quarterly, and annually will be described by the corporate procedure, but all internal financial reports must be developed with emphasis on meeting the responsibility and objective requirements of the new organizational structure. The new financial reports must be reviewed and approved by the subsidiary's management before implementation.

Reporting Requirements and Responsibility

The income statement and balance sheet responsibilities are summarized below and reflect a total integration, with the subsidiary losing its prior identity and becoming a plant location. This normally occurs when a vertical integration takes place. The centralized approach does not have to be totally integrated as outlined below, but modifications or different combinations of responsibilities can be established as long as the organizational structure and management's responsibilities are well defined.

The financial forecasting and reporting requirements and responsibilities for the income statement, balance sheet, and ratios should resemble the following outline:

Income Statement	Subsidiary	Corporate
Net Trade Sales		X
Cost of Goods Sold	X	
Gross Profit	X	X
Operating Expenses		
Marketing Expenses		X
Distribution Expenses	X	
Administration Expenses		X
Research Expenses	X	X
Other Income/(Expense)		X
Provision for Taxes		X
Employee Head Count	X	X
Capital Expenditures	X	X

Balance Sheet	Subsidiary	Corporate
Assets		
Petty Cash	X	
Cash		X
Accounts Receivable		X
Inventories	X	
Prepaid Expenses	X	X
Intercompany Transactions	X	X
Property, Plant, and Equipment	X	
Liabilities		
Accounts Payable	X	X
Accrued Liabilities		X
Accrued Payroll Costs		X
Accrued Taxes		X
Ratios		
Days Sales Outstanding		X
Inventory Turnover	X	
Return on Capital Employed		X

The new subsidiary will be responsible for developing and submitting the financial data associated with cost of goods sold, distribution expenses, and research expenses. The corporate office will be responsible for developing and submitting the remaining financial data as required and consolidating all financial information for reporting purposes. Planning, communication, and coordination are not only the key requirements for a successful financial forecasting cycle but also for the monthly, quarterly, and annual financial reporting requirements. To assist in this process, schedule formats are designed so that each location's financial data is prepared consistently and submitted to corporate in the same format so that the data can be combined as presented in Exhibit 2.2. This also assists management in the presentation, review, and approval of all financial data. This exhibit and those that follow are for the Example Manufacturing Company, which is a subsidiary of a larger corporation.

Exhibit 2.2 Example Manufacturing Company Consolidated Gross Profit Summary (Dollars in Thousands)

	Subsidiary		Corporate		Consolidated		Fav./ (Unfav.)
	Actual	Forecast	Actual	Forecast	Actual	Forecast	
Net trade sales	$	$	$10,000	$9,500	$10,000	$9,500	$ 500
Std. cost of sales			3,000	2,700	3,000	2,700	(300)
Std. gross profit			7,000	6,800	7,000	6,800	200
Percent of Sales			70.0%	71.6%	70.0%	71.6%	
Mfg. variances							
Spending	(250)	(300)			(250)	(300)	(50)
Absorption	150	175			150	175	25
Subtotal	(100)	(125)			(100)	(125)	(25)
Material variances							
Material usage	200	225			200	225	25
Yields	(150)	(175)			(150)	(175)	(25)
Subtotal	50	50			50	50	—

Purchase price var.	200	100			200	100	(100)
Total variances	150	25			150	25	(125)
Cost not in std.							
Scrap	200	250	100	120	300	370	70
Phys. inv. adjs.	100	100	50	30	150	130	(20)
Interplant freight	250	225			250	225	(25)
Development	250	220	50	45	300	265	(35)
Subtotal	800	795	200	195	1,000	990	(10)
Total variances and cost not in std.	950	820	200	195	1,150	1,015	(135)
Total cost of sales	950	820	3,200	2,895	4,150	3,715	(435)
Total gross profit	$ (950)	$ (820)	$ 6,800	$6,605	$ 5,850	$5,785	$ 65
Percent of sales	-%	-%	-%	-%	58.5%	60.9%	(2.4)%

RESPONSIBILITY REPORTING

Developing Financial Performance Criteria

As mentioned before, implementing the centralized approach will require the subsidiary's management to define the new elements of, as well as restate, prior financial reports so that consistent and relevant data will be available for corporate management review. Developing a financial reporting system to meet the objectives of the centralized approach requires a considerable amount of coordination and understanding between the financial and operational management combined with financial creativity. The major factor in designing the financial reporting system is to define the financial parameters that are critical to the subsidiary's performance. Both the corporate's and the subsidiary's management must take part in developing the financial parameters, as well as approve the financial reporting systems that will be utilized to present the financial results of the subsidiary. Examples of financial performance criteria are as follows:

1. Variances from standard manufacturing costs.
2. Number of months supply of inventory.
3. Variance from current forecast (plan).
4. Productivity indices.
5. Direct labor utilization.

After the benchmarks have been established, these financial performance criteria will be used by management to evaluate the short-term and long-term performance of the subsidiary. The criteria should not be changed or altered except to accommodate a significant change to the operation, such as a manufacturing process change, new products, or a consolidation of operations.

The performance parameters of a subsidiary must be evaluated and measured against a predetermined goal (forecast or budget) and past performance. *It is critical that the method and approach used to develop the performance parameters are consistently applied to the historical results as well as current period and forecasted financial data.* The historical operating performance of the subsidiary can be used to establish benchmarks to evaluate the short-term and long-term strategy of the subsidiary. During the process of developing the financial reporting system, every effort should be exercised to establish one set of financial statements that will meet both management teams' requirements. This will eliminate unnecessary duplication of work as well as prevent the release of conflicting financial data.

Once the performance criteria are developed and approved by management, then it is the responsibility of the finance management to develop the financial data base and report formats to be utilized in meeting the reporting requirements of the subsidiary. Both the subsidiary's and corporate's management will have an opportunity to review, change, and approve the new financial reporting system.

Financial Reporting Techniques

Some of the financial reporting techniques used to measure and evaluate the operating results of a subsidiary utilizing the centralized approach are as follows:

Operation's Highlights. Exhibit 2.3 represents a summary of the major factors that have an impact upon the operation. Gives subsidiary and corporate management a concise summary of the year-to-date operating results in comparison to the budget plan and prior-year actual. This summary should also include commentary that would explain significant deviations from the forecast and the prior-year results. Each item listed on this exhibit is a defined performance criteria.

Gross Profit Analysis. Exhibit 2.4 presents a summary explanation of the gross profit variance from forecast and identifies the marketing and operational impact, which are defined performance criteria. Product absorption, which is classified under the operations impact, can also be related to the marketing impact if there is a significant sales deviation from forecast. The marketing impact is the responsibility of corporate, while the subsidiary is responsible for the operations impact in the exhibit.

Gross Profit Statement. Exhibit 2.5 is a detail analysis of the gross profit results of the operation used by management to evaluate the total performance of the business unit excluding corporate's cost not in standard. This schedule is utilized by corporate finance to consolidate the gross profit results of the total corporation. Significant deviations from plan or prior-year actual are highlighted on this statement.

Operating Expenses. Exhibit 2.6 summarizes the subsidiary's actual spending of operating expenses versus forecast and prior-year actual for management's evaluation. This schedule is utilized by corporate finance to consolidate financial results. The deviation from forecast as well as the operating expenses as a percent of net trade sales are defined performance criteria.

EXHIBIT 2.3 *Example Manufacturing Company Subsidiary Operations Highlights (Dollars in Thousands)*

	Actual Year-to-Date	Current Forecast	Favorable/ (Unfavorable)	Prior Year
Net trade sales (a)	$ 10,000	$ 9,500	$ 500	$ 7,200
Standard gross profit	$ 7,000	$ 6,800	$ 200	$ 4,900
Percent of sales	70.0%	71.6%	(1.6)%	68.0%
Total gross profit	$ 6,050	$ 5,980	$ 70	$ 4,200
Percent of sales	60.5%	62.9%	(2.4)%	58.3%
Operating expenses	$ 1,400	$ 1,360	(40)	$ 1,100
Percent of sales	14.0%	14.3%	.3 %	15.3%
Head count	68	75	7	60
Gross inventory	$ 1,500	$ 1,350	$ (150)	$ 1,150
Number of months supply	5.3	5.4	.1	5.1
Capital spending	$ 325	$ 380	$ 55	$ 275
Units produced	5,200	4,900	300	3,750

(a) Corporate responsibility, but data are required to analyze the direction of the business and its impact on the subsidiary's operating results.

Exhibit 2.4   Example Manufacturing Company Subsidiary Gross
Profit Analysis (Dollars in Thousands)

Marketing Impact (a)		
Sales Impact		
Volume		$ 360 F
Price		(110) UF
Mix		(50) UF
Total marketing impact		200 F
Operations Impact		
Purchase price variance		(100) UF
Manufacturing variance		
Spending	$ (50) UF	
Product absorption	25 F	
Material usage	25 F	
Yields	(25) UF	(25) UF
Cost not in standard		
Development	(30) UF	
Scrap	50 F	
Interplant freight	(25) UF	(5) UF
Total operations impact		(130) UF
Total gross profit variance		$ 70 F
from forecast		

F = Favorable
UF = Unfavorable
(a) Corporate responsibility, but data are required to analyze the direction of the business and
its impact on the subsidiary's operating results.

Inventory Analysis.   Exhibit 2.7 presents the subsidiary's current investment in inventories to management as well as the current trend. The
number of months supply is a performance criteria and used by management to monitor and control the level of inventory in relation to future
sales.

Head Count Analysis.   Exhibit 2.8 presents the subsidiary's current head
count versus forecast and prior-year actual. Significant deviations from
the staffing plan by area is highlighted in this exhibit.

Depending on the responsibility and complexity of the subsidiary's operation, additional reports and schedules will be required, such as accounts
receivable analysis, capital spending by project, and so forth. Exhibits 2.3
to 2.8 basically reflect the reporting requirements of a separate plant location

Exhibit 2.5 Example Manufacturing Company Subsidiary Gross Profit Statement (Dollars in Thousands)

	Actual Year-to-Date	Current Forecast	Favorable/ (Unfavorable)	Prior Year
Gross trade sales				
Product line A	$ 6,450	$ 6,020	$ 430	$ 4,300
Product line B	3,700	3,600	100	3,000
Total gross sales	10,150	9,620	530	7,300
Less cash discounts	150	120	(30)	(100)
Net trade sales	10,000	9,500	500	7,200
Standard cost of sales				
Product line A	1,520	1,500	(20)	1,300
Product line B	1,480	1,200	(280)	1,000
Total standard cost of sales	3,000	2,700	(300)	2,300
Standard gross profit	7,000	6,800	200	4,900
Percent of sales	70.0%	71.6%	(1.6)%	68.0%

Variances from standard costs

Purchase price	200	100	(100)	75
Manufacturing	(50)	(75)	(25)	25
Total variances	150	25	(125)	100
Adjusted gross profit	6,850	6,775	75	4,800
Percent of sales	68.5%	71.3%	(2.6)%	66.7%
Costs not in standard				
Inventory adjustments	100	100	–	100
Scrap	200	250	50	100
Development	250	220	(30)	225
Interplant freight	250	225	(25)	175
Total cost not in standard	800	795	(5)	600
Total cost of sales	3,950	3,520	(430)	3,000
Percent of sales	39.5%	37.1%	(2.4)%	41.7%
Total gross profit	$ 6,050	$ 5,980	$ 70	$ 4,200
Percent of sales	60.5%	62.9%	(2.4)%	58.3%

(a) Corporate responsibility, but data are required to analyze the direction of the business and its impact on the subsidiary's operating results.

Exhibit 2.6   Example Manufacturing Company Subsidiary Operating Expenses (Dollars in Thousands)

	Actual Year-to-Date	Current Forecast	Favorable/ (Unfavorable)	Prior Year
Distribution	$ 200	$ 190	$ (10)	$ 140
Freight	300	270	(30)	220
Personnel	150	160	10	120
Finance	250	260	10	200
Research	500	480	(20)	420
Total operating expenses	$1,400	$1,360	$ (40)	$1,100
Percent of net trade sales	14.0%	14.3%	.3%	15.3%

where the marketing, administrative, and research responsibilities were consolidated with corporate at the time of the acquisition.

Income Statement Analysis

From time to time corporate management will request an income statement analysis of the business unit that will include the direct manufacturing costs and expenses of the subsidiary as well as sales and operating expenses in-

Exhibit 2.7   Example Manufacturing Company Subsidiary Inventory Analysis (Dollars in Thousands)

Inventory Balances	Current Month Actual	Prior Month Actual	Current Forecast	Beginning of Year (a)
Raw material	$ 750	$ 500	$ 500	$ 600
Work-in-process	250	400	350	250
Finished goods	500	350	500	300
Total gross inventories	1,500	1,250	1,350	1,150
Reserves	(150)	(135)	(125)	(150)
Total net inventories	$1,350	$1,115	$1,225	$1,000
Number of months supply				
Gross	5.3	5.0	5.4	5.1
Net	4.8	4.5	4.5	4.4

(a) Prior-year inventory balances at current year standard costs.

Exhibit 2.8   Example Manufacturing Company Subsidiary Head Count

	Current Actual	Current Forecast	Increase/ (Decrease)	Prior Year
Manufacturing	49	54	(5)	43
Materials management	3	5	(2)	4
Distribution	3	2	1	2
Finance	6	6	—	5
Personnel	2	2	—	2
Research	5	6	(1)	4
Total	68	75	(7)	60

curred at corporate for the benefit of the business unit. When the centralized approach to management and financial reporting is implemented, certain expenses are not readily identifiable to the business unit, especially if corporate is the marketing arm for several subsidiaries. The first step in performing this exercise is to identify the direct expenses at both locations in the following manner:

	Subsidiary	Corporate
Net trade sales		X
Standard cost of sales		X
Manufacturing variances and cost not in standard	X	
Marketing expenses		X
Freight	X	
Research expenses	X	X

Net trade sales and standard cost of sales are derived from the sales reporting system at corporate. The manufacturing variances and costs-not-in-standard are presented in the subsidiary's financial reports. Direct marketing expenses will include selling commissions, advertising, sales promotions, and product management costs that are identifiable to the business unit. A separate cost center at the subsidiary will capture all freight costs associated with the business unit sales. Direct research activity can take place at both locations depending on how the research function is organized. A product development staff can be located at the subsidiary, while the basic research is performed by the corporate staff.

Exhibit 2.9 Example Manufacturing Company Consolidated Income Statement Format (Dollars in Thousands)

	Current Actual	Current Forecast	Fav./ (Unfav.)	Prior Year
Net trade sales	$10,000	$ 9,500	$ 500	$ 7,200
Standard cost of sales	3,000	2,700	(300)	2,300
Standard gross profit	7,000	6,800	200	4,900
Percent of sales	70.0%	71.6%	(1.6)%	68.0%
Direct expenses				
Manufacturing variances	150	25	(125)	100
Costs not in standard	800	795	(5)	600
Freight	300	270	(30)	220
Selling commissions (corp.)	300	285	(15)	210
Distribution	200	190	(10)	140
Personnel	150	160	10	120
Finance	250	260	10	200
Research	500	480	(20)	420

Total direct expenses	2,650	2,465	(185)	2,010
Percent of sales	26.5%	26.0%	(.5)%	27.9%
Controllable margin	4,350	4,335	15	2,890
Percent of sales	43.5%	45.6%	(2.1)%	40.1%
Indirect and allocated expenses (corp.)				
Marketing	2,250	2,300	50	1,575
Distribution	275	255	(20)	195
Administration	425	450	25	300
Research	250	225	(25)	175
Total indirect and allocated expenses	3,200	3,230	30	2,245
Percent of sales	32.0%	34.0%	2.0%	31.2%
Operating profit	1,150	1,105	45	645
Percent of sales	11.5%	11.6%	.1%	8.9%
Provision for taxes on income	575	552	23	322
Net income	$ 575	$ 553	$ 22	$ 323
Percent of sales	5.8%	5.8%	—%	4.5%

The more difficult task is to identify and allocate the indirect (overhead) expenses incurred at corporate associated with the subsidiary's business unit. Percentage of effort can be obtained from the sales force, marketing staff, and the research staff. A research project reporting system can assist in identifying both the direct and indirect research expenses. Distribution expenses can be allocated based on the subsidiary's sales volume (shipment) or percentage of effort if this product line requires special handling or service. Percentage of effort or cost as a percent of sales approach can be utilized in allocating administration expenses. A detailed understanding of the business unit's operation and the financial reporting system combined with creativity is necessary in developing the assumptions associated with determining the indirect costs to be allocated to business units for income statement presentation.

Since the business unit's income statement is not based totally on identifiable costs, the formats can be modified to meet managements' requirements as presented in Exhibit 2.9.

This format assists management in evaluating the financial performance of the business unit from a controllable margin and net income perspective. The current financial results are compared against the current forecast as well as prior-year historical results. Controllable margin represents the financial results of the subsidiary's business activities that are identifiable and controllable either at the subsidiary or corporate level and reflects the profit remaining to cover the indirect and allocated costs. The method and approach used to develop the business unit income statement must be properly documented in a compendium so that in the future this analysis can be prepared in a consistent fashion for management's evaluation.

Another approach is to develop a business unit income statement utilizing the variable and fixed-cost (cost–volume–profit) concept. This method would be similar to the approach described above, however, cost of sales would be split into variable and fixed costs. The variable cost would be classified in the income statement as a direct expense, while the fixed costs would be classified as an indirect or allocated expense. Either approach implemented consistently can be used as a criterion to measure the business unit's financial performance.

CHECKLIST

General

1. Meet with the new subsidiary's management to discuss the following:
    (a) Management philosophy

    (b)   Organizational structure

    (c)   Financial systems and procedures

2. Define management's philosophy—centralization versus decentralization.

3. Develop the subsidiary's organizational structure in line with the centralized approach.

4. Communicate all aspects of the centralized approach and the new subsidiary's organization structure to all employees.

5. Arrange a visit by the new subsidiary's management to another subsidiary of the corporation to review operating and financial procedures as well as organization structure and responsibilities.

Integration Program

1. Evaluate the subsidiary's current financial procedures and computerized systems.

2. Identify the financial computerized systems that can be integrated with corporate:

    (a)   General ledger.

    (b)   Accounts payable.

    (c)   Payroll/benefits.

    (d)   Sales order processing.

    (e)   Accounts receivable.

    (f)   Inventory management and control.

    (g)   Fixed assets.

    (h)   Budgeting.

3. Define computer hardware and software requirements and associated costs at both locations.

4. Evaluate current system programs and identify applicable programming changes.

5. Establish a training program for the subsidiary's personnel.

6. Identify and resolve all system's problems encountered.

7. Evaluate system's staffing requirements and priorities.

8. Develop a systems integration program and obtain management's approval.

9. Identify financial procedures that can be consolidated with corporate:

    (a)   Cash management.

    (b)   Cash disbursements.

(c)   Expenditure delegation.

(d)   Inventory valuation.

(e)   Intercompany transactions.

(f)   Capitalization of fixed assets.

(g)   Depreciation of fixed assets.

(h)   Financial reporting.

10.   Evaluate the impact this approach will have on the subsidiary's financial procedures.

11.   Identify and resolve all procedural problems encountered.

12.   Prepare and document all new financial procedures.

13.   Develop an integration program that must coincide with the system's integration program.

14.   Obtain management's approval of all new procedures as well as the integration program.

15.   Identify individual responsibility for each area of the financial systems and procedures integration program, including the timing of events.

Responsibility Reporting

1.   Obtain an understanding of the subsidiary's operational and financial systems and procedures.

2.   Define the financial performance criteria for the subsidiary in accordance with the centralized approach and organizational structure.

3.   Obtain corporate and subsidiary managements' approval of the financial performance criteria.

4.   Develop a financial reporting system based on the financial performance criteria and organizational structure.

5.   Review financial reporting system with management in order to obtain feedback and approval.

6.   Implement the new subsidiary's financial reporting system.

7.   Identify what financial information will be required by corporate on the date of the acquisition as well as monthly, quarterly, and annually.

8.   Establish financial reporting deadlines.

9.   Identify the subsidiary's historical financial data that will be required for financial reporting purposes.

10.   Establish the financial forecast requirements for the subsidiary.

three

A DECENTRALIZED APPROACH

William J. Delayo, MBA

CONTENTS

DECENTRALIZATION

Decentralization is an organizational process whereby *autonomy is given to lower levels* of management and subunits. This means that there is a downward shifting of responsibilities in the organization in order to complete a task or run an operation. Decentralization is referred to by many as not only a form of organization but *a way or life*—an ideal style of management.

From a practical standpoint decentralization means the acquired company maintains its identity and the management is given a high level of autonomy. A review of the major differences between the centralized and decentralized approaches discussed in the following sections will highlight the many ways in which the acquired company retains its independent attributes. Internal financial reporting within the acquired company may remain intact; however, the parent organization will need key financial and operational information to satisfy public and top management reporting requirements. The acquired company will be viewed by the acquiring company's top management as a separate entity and its management will be evaluated on bottom-line results.

The types of industry that a company is operating in, as well as the technology or nature of its product lines, must be kept in mind because they could have an influence on the degree of decentralization that may be appropriate for an acquired entity.

Problems and Opportunities

Companies that choose to follow the decentralized mode of operation have reached that decision after concluding that a *centralized operation is less effective*. However, there are problems in a decentralized operation. For example, if the decisions are of such significance to require parent management involvement, then these situations and decisions must be handled at that level. Thus a major advantage of decentralization—prompt decisions made on the local level—is lost. An example of such a situation would be a decision required on a capital project that has anticipated costs in excess of

Grateful acknowledgment is given to Mr. Kevin P. Dwyer, MBA, and Ms. Florence A. McLean, CPA, Managers of Financial Analysis and Financial Procedures, respectively, for their extensive contributions to Chapter 3.

the approval levels of local management. Delays in the decision could make it difficult for local management to respond promptly to competitive threats.

The opportunities that are afforded operating units within a decentralized organization are many. From the human side, such a management process provides for the fulfillment of self-expression and needs, the opportunity for independence, and the satisfaction for the acquired company's management in the achievement of its accomplishments. Further, in a decentralized environment ordinarily there is a minimization in the layers of management and a broader span of control. Consequently, there is not a buildup of the layers of management that could insulate top executives from the problems. Such a process uses all levels of personnel in arriving at decisions throughout the organization. Managers are developed and potential achieved more rapidly.

Advantages of Decentralization

Organizations that accept the decentralized approach to be more productive obviously conclude that the advantages outweigh the disadvantages. Some principle advantages are:

1. Local management of the acquired company is in the best position to make timely decisions.
2. The acquired company's management is responsible for using its initiative and imagination in developing strategic plans.
3. Realizing they are evaluated on bottom-line results, the local management personnel will be more dynamic in striving to achieve their objectives.
4. Opportunities for developing an increased pool of management talent for the entire business entity is enhanced because more individuals have a chance to be involved in profit-based decisions at the local level.

In a highly decentralized operation the freedom to adjust to changing situations is quite evident. This requires voluntary coordination and significant information sharing on everyone's part so they can adjust to the needs of others. For this sharing to be effective, objectives must be clarified and clearly communicated. Individuals will voluntarily work together if they understand and are concerned about the objectives and operational results of the unit. Objectives and goals are a necessary prerequisite for control standards. In a decentralized environment the freedom to adjust must be accomplished without the loss of control. Internal control systems are discussed later in this chapter.

Special Management Problems

Decentralization requires capable individuals who can accept delegation and the responsibilities that accompany it, as well as the general supervision from the acquiring company that is essential. All managers must share a common understanding of the objectives of the organization or else such autonomy can lead to dysfunctional operations. The need for high-quality management individuals cannot be stressed enough in order for decentralization to work effectively.

There are hidden costs inherent in a decentralized environment. Duplication of staff skills as well as added costs of developing necessary information controls to keep top management appraised of results are merely two such items. The greatest drain on potential operating profits is lack of coordination between sister companies, where benefits to one may be more than offset by a greater loss of benefits to another.

In order to deal with personnel problems, unrest, or uncertainty, that necessarily develop as the result of a merger or acquisition, communication with all parties is the key. It is necessary that a well-planned communications program be put in place as soon as the acquisition is completed. Such a program should have at least three main objectives:

1. Educating all major groups of employees as to the effect of the merger on them relative to the continuation of management, wage scales and union affiliations, and other personnel/employee benefits type questions.
2. Providing an understanding to all employees as to the benefits of the merger from the standpoint of both companies involved so that they may be aware of the product mix, management philosophies, and needs of both organizations.
3. A genuine concern on the part of the acquiring company's management should be evident regarding the welfare of the acquired company's employees by demonstrating a true human sensitivity to their needs.

An education and orientation program is outlined for individuals within the financial organization in the following section.

ORIENTATION OF ACQUIRED FINANCIAL MANAGEMENT

Importance in a Decentralized Organization

Sensitivity to people's needs is of utmost importance in the acquisition of a company, particularly if that acquired company is going to be managed in the future in a decentralized style of management. Although the decentralized approach allows the acquired management to retain much control, having to report to a higher unit for the first time can have a dramatic effect on the overall morale of the acquired company. It is extremely important to ensure that proper communications are made to all levels within the acquired company. As discussed in an earlier section, communications should relate the reasons for the acquisition, the benefits that will come to all parties, and, ultimately, an attempt to express an understanding of the perceptions that the personnel of the newly acquired company may have. Consequently, very thorough orientations for the financial management of the acquired company should be conducted. In this manner they can be quickly informed, on an overview basis, of the expectations for the reporting systems required by the acquiring company.

Levels of Management Oriented

Depending on the size of the acquired company, several levels of orientation programs may be required for the financial management of the organization. Obviously, the chief financial person and key financial and accounting managers are the primary group of individuals that should receive this orientation. It is critical that the acquired company's financial management fully understand what is expected of it. These expectations should be established early. Further, they should become familiar with the areas within the parent's financial organization to go to for assistance should difficulties be encountered. Depending on the size of the acquired company, it may be possible to have an orientation of the entire financial group.

Key Areas for Orientation

Procedures and Policies. This initial area of orientation would encompass a complete overview of the corporate structure, the parent company structure, and, more specifically, the organizational setup of the financial division within each. A review of the various information and reporting systems of the acquiring company will be necessary. The numerous policies governing management reporting requirements, as well as the public reporting needs of the parent, should be explained so that the acquired company's financial management has a thorough understanding of these obligations. Further, a thorough review should be conducted of the process involved in generating and issuing the various procedures that outline the details required for periodic reporting by the acquired company to the parent.

The information services organization should also explain how the data is received, input, and reported on as a result of the submissions from the various affiliates to the parent. Any systems services such as modeling capabilities, and/or computer graphics capabilities available to the acquired company's financial management for their potential future use should be explained.

Financial Reporting and Analysis. A complete review is necessary of both the internal and external cyclical reporting requirements. In addition to the normal income statement and balance sheet components of reporting, other areas that may be worthy of elaboration for the acquired company's personnel would be segments of business reporting, current cost information, impact of FASB and SEC regulations, cost reduction and profit improvement items, and head count/productivity measurement. The parent's organizational structure of the reporting and analysis areas should be explained, as well as the respective departmental missions and objectives. It is important to communicate that the analyses that are provided to the parent company usually are at the request of the parent's top management. Another key area that must be understood by the acquired company's financial management is the development of the strategic plan. Especially that such a long-term plan is not reviewed precisely as a detailed forecast but rather reviewed in a broad sense. Again, it is important for the acquired financial management to know if the parent's financial analysis area is available for assistance in completing capital evaluation projects, various competitor analyses, lease versus buy analyses, or other computer modeling techniques.

Compensation and Benefits. As mentioned previously, the morale of the acquired company is likely to be impacted by the acquisition. One area of obvious concern will be compensation. The financial personnel of the acquired company should be made aware of the benefits and compensation packages that could be made available from the parent organization. Further, it is important for them to understand the role that job evaluations play in the salary structure, a structure that can be modified based on surveys throughout the industry in which the parent operates. The personnel or administrative functions would be the areas directly involved in explaining these issues and in coordinating any changes that may be contemplated.

Tax and Treasury Functions. The financial management of the local organization of the acquired company will be expected to understand the tax ramifications resulting from the acquisition. The parent's tax department should review any tax developments, including new legislation, cases, and rulings. The reports required to be made directly to the parent's tax department should be reviewed to ensure proper adherence in order to comply with timely tax filings. With regard to treasury functions, it will be necessary to review cash management and intercompany lending policies so that the acquired company's financial management has an understanding of the limitations and approval levels in this area.

Auditing. As in any major corporation made up of numerous subsidiaries, there is a staff of internal auditors. Their primary role is to evaluate the management and accounting internal control systems within the subsidiaries on an ongoing and recurring basis. A more detailed discussion of internal control systems and the role of the auditors is given later in this chapter. It is important for the auditing department to review the objectives of their audit work, the various types of audits that are conducted, and a brief overview of the audit process itself.

International Operations. The financial management of the acquired company should be made aware of international operations that are also affiliates of the parent. It would be helpful for them to know the structure of the international organization and the various technical services provided through the parent for current or potential international operations of the acquired company. The parent also may have established an export division through which all shipments are made. A review of the physical facilities, the various planning and ordering cycles, any invoicing or information flows required, and the necessary communications network to fulfill the missions of the international organizations should be explained thoroughly.

Summary

The orientation of the acquired financial management is important to the effective integration of an acquired company. An orientation guide developed by the parent so the acquired financial management could identify key areas of importance to it would be beneficial. The amount of time devoted and the amount of detail covered will depend on the caliber and talent of acquired financial management. It is of utmost importance to conduct an orientation as soon as possible after the acquisition is completed. A timetable for the orientation and, if possible, visits to other affiliates should be arranged for the acquired company's financial management. This planning is critical if the integration of the decentralized style of management into the acquired company is to be successful.

MEETING FINANCING NEEDS OF THE ACQUIRED BUSINESS

During the various stages of investigation of a potential acquisition, the topic of financing the acquisition is reviewed. As most research will indicate, the methods of payment for an acquisition can take the form of cash, stock, or a combination of both. The use of cash can trigger various forms of financing. This section, however, will deal with the financing needs of the acquired business after the acquisition, that is, ongoing cash requirements, which usually take the form of increases in working capital (receivables and inventories), capital expenditures, or in the case of an unprofitable acquisition, covering losses from operations.

Loans

A common method of financing operations is through parent company loans to subsidiaries. Such loans could be treated similar to outside loans, including interest payments and repayment terms. Interest should be based on a financial rate, that is, borrowing rate, and should be charged monthly.

Recapitalization

Recapitalization is the process by which a parent loan on the acquired's books is eliminated and the total amount transferred to the acquired's capital account. This becomes a capital infusion that is not likely to be repaid.

Intercompany Pricing

Another method of financing operations of the newly acquired company is through intercompany pricing. If the acquired affiliate charges the receiving affiliate a price for its products that exceeds their respective costs, the acquired company will increase its net income and therefore provide cash. The financing in this case is provided by the receiving affiliate. This is the same source of financing that is received from outside customers when the market price for the product exceeds the cost to produce it.

Dividend Payments

The parent company expects future cash flows from the acquisition. Obviously, the amount and timing will depend on the profitability of the acquired company as well as other factors. There is no set requirement for such payments because each acquisition must be considered independently. (Cash flows to the parent company are commonly referred to as dividends.)

Dividend guidelines should consider future cash needs of the subsidiary, but might include the following conditions as examples of payment terms:

Amount should equal 50% of net income

No dividend if retained earnings are negative

With International acquisitions, the dividend plan may be subject to local governmental restrictions that can vary widely. For example, the following three countries and their respective dividend restrictions highlight the vast differences from one country to another:

Germany: no restrictions

Philippines: no restrictions if debt–equity ratio does not exceed 55 : 45, and if dividends are not financed through local borrowings.

Dominican Republic: The maximum annual gross dividend that can be paid is limited to 18% of registered U.S. dollar investment. Dividends are further limited to profits generated from locally manufactured products.

The guidelines for international acquisitions should follow those outlined for domestic companies whenever possible.

CORPORATE MANAGEMENT REPORTING

Purpose (Uniformity and Consistency)

The primary purpose of a management reporting system is to provide useful financial information to management, stockholders, and the public. These financial results include the reporting of actual results (i.e., monthly, quarterly, and year-end) and the reporting of business plans.

The reporting of results to satisfy stockholders and the public in the United States is determined by three rule-making bodies: the Financial Accounting Standards Board (FASB), the Securities and Exchange Commission (SEC), and the U.S. Congress; whereas management reporting needs are determined by each company. Management reporting is necessary to provide information to prepare the company's business plan, assess the company's potential to achieve the plan's objective, to make judgments about alternative courses of action, to measure actual performance against the plan, and to take corrective action when necessary.

The parent company would therefore define the key information that is needed from the acquired company to fulfill all types of reporting requirements. At a minimum, the parent company may only require key balance sheet and income statement items such as cash, marketable securities, inventories, receivables, capital expenditures, net trade sales, and net income on a monthly basis and a complete balance sheet and income statement on a quarterly basis. In a more comprehensive system considerably more data, including budget to actual comparisons, forecasts, and capital expenditure plans would be required.

Local Management Reporting of International Affiliates

Multinational companies must also meet reporting requirements that are established either by governments or private regulatory boards in the countries in which they conduct their business. Some of these reporting requirements are similar to U.S. requirements, however, differences do exist. In 1973 the International Accounting Standards Committee (IASC) was formed to reconcile differing accounting practices among its various member countries. The statements issued by IASC have addressed items that are already accepted accounting principles in the United States. However, there are no international uniform accounting principles. Thus multinational companies may request that the acquired company financial information to be used for public reporting be prepared in accordance with U.S. GAAP. Alternately, the request could be for the local company to identify all items not in accordance witn U.S. GAAP.

Key Reporting Procedures

To achieve uniformity in reporting, to comply with regulatory requirements, and to satisfy management's reporting needs, the parent company should establish reporting procedures. Reporting procedures should be comprehensive and concise and cover reporting guidelines and formats for all appropriate cycles. These procedures must be clearly understood by the acquired company.

Reporting cycles—The procedure includes business plan and actual result cycles. Depending on the complexity and the size of the organization, business plans may be required annually or several times during the year. Business plans are essential since they are used to develop the company's goals (growth, profitability) and provide alternative actions. The actual reporting cycles may include monthly management reports and quarterly as well as year-end stockholders' and management reports.

Reporting procedures for these cycles may include *balance sheet reporting* (see Exhibit 3.1). The procedure should define balance sheet classifications and the various balance sheet items that should be reported in each classification. For example *reporting line 100—Cash–Non-Interest-Bearing—* should include all cash in company bank accounts not earning interest or in transit to company bank accounts as well as all imprest petty cash funds.

*Reporting line 134—Construction in Progress—*should include all costs incurred as of the statement date to construct buildings and machinery and/ or equipment not yet placed in service.

On Exhibit 3.1 the line number designates each item that should be included in the balance sheet report. This line number designation is provided to facilitate the data input and processing of the reports by the parent.

*Reporting Net Income and Retained Earnings—*The procedure should define the various income and expense items, when they should be recognized, and how to report them. For example, *trade sales* should include sales, net of returns, and allowances to all customers other than intercompany sales. *Transportation costs* should include all outbound transportation costs of moving merchandise from a warehouse to the customer and for moving finished merchandise from a manufacturing point to a warehouse at another location from which it is ultimately to be distributed to the customer. The cost of the traffic department, where there is such a separate department that has responsibility for administration of freight costs, should also be included in this category.

One possible format for a statement of income and retained earnings with appropriate line designations for data input is shown in Exhibit 3.2.

In addition to reporting revenues, cost, and balance sheet items, ratios may be required by management to evaluate the affiliate's actual performance against its goals. Statistical ratios are used to highlight and understand trends. These trends may then be compared to forecast, prior-period actual results, or industry averages. These ratios, in conjunction with the income statement and balance sheet, provide management with information with which to evaluate the affiliate, identify deviations from objectives, and take corrective actions where appropriate. Statistical ratios and other data that may be used include the following:

Number of days' sales in trade accounts receivable is used to measure the average collection period of sales.

Accounts receivable aging is performed to determine an approximation of the net realizable value of the accounts receivable balance.

Exhibit 3.1 Balance Sheet Data Reporting Form

Assets	Line No.	Amount
	6–8	9–19
Current assets		
Cash and cash items	100	
Marketable securities, at cost, which approximates market value	101	
Accounts receivable, trade, less allowances	102	
Inventories	103	
Prepaid expenses and other receivables	104	
Total current assets	105	
Marketable securities, noncurrent	106	
Land and land improvements	107	
Buildings and building equipment	108	
Machinery and equipment	109	
Construction in progress	110	
Less accumulated depreciation and amortization	111	
Property, plant and equipment	112	
Other assets	113	
Total assets	114	

Liabilities and Stockholders' Equity

Current liabilities		
Loans and notes payable	120	
Accounts payable, trade	121	
Miscellaneous accounts payable	122	
Taxes on income	123	
Salaries, wages, and commissions	124	
Miscellaneous taxes	125	
Miscellaneous accrued liabilities	126	
Total current liabilities	130	
Long-term debt	131	
Certificates of extra compensation	132	
Deferred investment tax credits	133	
Other liabilities and deferrals	134	
Minority interests in international subsidiaries	135	
Stockholders' equity		
Preferred stock	137	
Common stock	138	
Additional capital	139	
Retained earnings	140	
Total stockholders' equity	141	
Total liabilities and stockholders' equity	150	

Exhibit 3.2   Statement of Income and Retained Earnings

Line Name	Line No. 6–8	Amount 9–19
Revenues		
Sales to customers	201	
Other revenues		
Interest income	202	
Royalties and miscellaneous	203	
Total revenues	205	
Costs and expenses		
Cost of products sold	210	
Selling, distribution, and		
administrative expenses	211	
Research expenses	212	
Interest expense	213	
Interest expense capitalized	214	
Other expenses	215	
Total costs and expenses	220	
Earnings before provision for taxes on income	225	
Provision for taxes on income	230	
Net earnings	240	
Retained earnings at beginning of period	245	
Cash dividends paid	250	
Retained earnings at end of period	260	

Number of months' business in gross inventories is used to determine the adequacy of the current inventory level to satisfy future sales.

Employee head count data is used to manage employment costs, to determine the adequacy of the staffing, and to measure employee productivity.

Price and volume changes are used to explain and identify changes in sales between periods (e.g., forecast to forecast, forecast to actual, or actual to actual) and to what extent the sales change is due to price changes or volume changes.

Working Capital

Another area of concern to management, creditors, and other financial statement users is the amount of available working capital. This is a measure of a unit's ability to pay liabilities within the ordinary operating cycle of the business and should, therefore, be monitored to ascertain that the components of working capital are being used efficiently.

Sales/Income Reporting

Individual Subsidiary Results. The income statement is by far the most widely used measurement of operating performance. Therefore, each subsidiary should report to management a full income statement including cost of goods sold, all marketing expenses, distribution expenses, and all other expense categories, as well as a contingency in any forecast period. The example format of a statement of income and retained earnings is presented in Exhibit 3.2.

Product Lines/Groups. If within a given subsidiary several different products and/or product lines are sold, the sales of these products should be reported to corporate management. Exhibit 3.3 presents a suggested form to report this data. At this detailed level the reporting of sales only would be sufficient.

Exhibit 3.3 Sales by Product Line Report

	Product Number	Annual Sales 19___
Consumer Products		
Shampoos	01	_____
Colognes	02	_____
Lotions	03	_____
Deodorants	04	_____
Total Toiletries	10	_____
Toothbrushes	11	_____
Dental Floss	12	_____
Total Dental Products	20	_____
Total Consumer Products (Lines 10 & 20)	30	_____
Pharmaceutical Products		
Contraceptives	31	_____
Therapeutics	32	_____
Dermatologicals	33	_____
Analgesics	34	_____
Total Human Pharmaceuticals	40	_____
Total Veterinary Products	50	_____
Total Pharmaceuticals (Lines 40 & 50)	60	_____
Total Sales (Lines 30 & 60)	100	_____

An abbreviated income statement is required for the major product lines. Referring to Exhibit 3.3, the major product lines are identified as Total Toiletries, Total Dental Products, Total Consumer Products, Total Human Pharmaceutical Products, Total Veterinary Products, and Total Pharmaceutical Products. The form presented in Exhibit 3.4 depicts the expense items that are required for management reporting.

Segments of Business.   Segments of business reporting is described in FAS 14, which requires that any combination of similar product groups that represents 10% or more of total company sales should be disclosed. As far as management reporting is concerned, each subsidiary should report sales and income data on a major product line basis. This information is summarized in a segment grouping. For example, referring again to Exhibit 3.4, the major segment classifications are Total Consumer Products and Total Pharmaceutical Products. This data is disclosed to the public and appears in the annual report.

Geographic Areas.   Geographic reporting of financial data provides management with a valuable decision-making tool. Depending on the business, it may be useful to capture data at a country level and then by continent or region. For example, a company may have subsidiaries in Europe and South America as well as the United States. Sales and income data for each of these geographic areas will enable corporate management to differentiate between regions and their performance. Further, reporting only by the segments of business may not identify significant problems or opportunities because subsidiaries operating primarily in one segment may have diverse locations.

Price/Volume/Currency.   The nature of the components of sales increases/decreases is important for management to know. The components are price and volume. Some companies also identify product mix as a separate component. In multinational companies there is also a currency component.

Other Management Reports

In addition to the items enumerated earlier management may also use other financial data and ratios to evaluate the affiliate's operating results or to set objectives. These other management reports may include:

Cost Reduction Programs.   This type of reporting would be useful in identifying areas in which the affiliate's resources may be used more

Exhibit 3.4 Sales and Income Report by Product Group

Product Group	Line Number	Sales	Cost of Goods Sold	Expenses					Interest	Other (Inc) Exp.	IBT	Tax Prov.	Net Income
				Marketing	R&D	Other Commercial	Contingency (Fcst. Only)						
Toiletries	10												
Dental products	20												
Total consumer prod. (Lines 10 & 20)	30												
Human pharm.	40												
Veterinary prod.	50												
Total pharm. (Lines 40 & 50)	60												
Total company	100												

efficiently. Actions that could result in such changes may include the reduction of costs in any area of the business through the elimination of redundancies and change in production methods.

Return on Capital Employed. This type of reporting is useful as a measure of the operating efficiency of the affiliate since it indicates how the capital is used in the earnings process. For this purpose, income and capital would not include items classified as nonoperating income or assets.

Inflation Reporting. Inflation reporting resulted from the criticism of historical cost statements as a reliable measure of the affiliate's performance and its management of the resources. Inflation reporting may be useful in assessing future cash flows, the erosion of operating capability, and financial performance.

Report of Capital Expenditures. This is useful in providing management with information on current programs and cost estimates to complete projects that are in process. This is necessary because management has to control all investment spending to ensure that funds are properly used.

Net Asset Exposure. The amount of foreign assets/liabilities that are at risk to foreign exchange rate changes is useful to management.

ACCOUNTING ALTERNATIVES

To ensure comparability between financial statements, the accounting rules promulgated by the FASB or the SEC usually prescribe one method of reporting or accounting for certain transactions. In others, however, these rule-making bodies allow some flexibility in accounting. Some of the transactions that may be reported and accounted for under different methods include inventory, depreciation, and investment tax credits.

Inventory Valuation

The inventory cost reported in the financial statements may be determined by using such inventory valuation methods as first-in first-out (FIFO), average, and last-in first-out (LIFO). In choosing the method to use, management should select the one that is applicable to the business and that is more appropriate in determining production costs. This decision should be made only after each of these alternative methods have been properly analyzed as to the effect on the business.

The FIFO cost method recognizes the earliest cost as the cost of production. In periods of high inflation this inventory costing method has the effect of showing low costs of sales and high income. The LIFO inventory costing method has a reverse effect of showing high costs of sales and reduced income and may be appropriate if high inflation is anticipated.

Depreciation Methods

Depreciation methods may be categorized as a function of time (i.e., based on an estimated useful life rather than how the asset is used) and/or a function of use or depletion. Depreciation methods that are a function of time include the straight-line method, declining balance method, and the sum of the years' digits method. Depreciation methods that are a function of use include the units of production method and the hours of use or mileage method. The depreciation method which is selected should:

1. Allocate the asset cost in a systematic manner.
2. Be applied consistently from period to period.
3. Match expense and revenues.
4. Produce reliable data for product and service costs.
5. Be most useful to management.

In addition to the different methods that may be used for book purposes, companies will use the methods allowed by the tax laws. The methods allowed include the double declining balance method, the depreciation of assets over a shorter length of time than would be used for book purposes, and for more recently required assets the Accelerated Cost Recovery System (ACRS) method. These methods are allowed by the government to encourage companies to invest their tax savings in capital projects.

Investment Tax Credit (ITC)

The investment tax credit, which is allowed under U.S. tax rules, may be reported in the financial statements in either of two ways: the flow-through method or the deferred method. Under the flow-through method the full amount of the ITC is reported as a reduction of federal income taxes in the year the eligible assets are placed in service, whereas the deferred method recognizes the ITC benefit over the productive life of the eligible assets. Managements that use the deferred method believe that the credit is earned over the life of the asset rather than when the asset is placed in service.

Financial statements should be prepared on a consistent basis for each reporting period. Since there are accounting alternatives, consistency may not be achieved if the accounting methods used by the acquired company are different from those used by the parent company. To achieve consistency, the parent company should communicate its accounting methods to the acquired company. In the event the acquired company is not able to conform to the parent's accounting methods, adjustments, if significant, should be made to the consolidated financial statements by the parent.

INTERNAL CONTROL SYSTEMS

Importance in a Decentralized Environment

Internal controls are needed in all companies. However, the level of internal controls from one company to another can be quite different for a number of reasons, such as management attitude, type of industry, and whether the company is publicly owned or not. Setting up proper internal controls in a newly acquired company is extremely important and must be implemented as soon as practicable. Even though the acquired company may have a system of internal controls, they will relate to its operation, not to its relationship with the parent.

A decentralized style of management allows the management of each business unit to operate autonomously. This presents the manager with the opportunity to act as an entrepreneur and therefore utilize his business knowledge and creativity to the fullest. The decentralized style of management does, however, require formal internal controls that safeguard against the potential for uncontrolled behavior inherent in this style of organization. This is not to say that internal controls are not necessary for a centralized management style, but given the different attributes of each style, internal controls take on a very significant role with decentralized management.

Internal Control Defined

Internal control includes the organizational plan and methods and measures used to safeguard assets, check accounting data for correctness, and provide for adherence to managerial policies.

Internal Auditing

Although line management has the responsibility to implement internal controls, the internal auditors are charged with the responsibility of overseeing and reviewing those controls, as well as checking the accuracy of data, promoting operational efficiency, and safeguarding assets. In addition, the internal auditors assist with the orientation of the acquired company's personnel by providing interpretations of internal procedures and reporting practices.

Specific Controls

Internal controls can be broken down into two categories: those controls that deal with the day-to-day operation of the firm and those controls that are aimed at corporatewide goals. In a decentralized environment the day-to-day controls are handled by the affiliate. They would include such things as invoice approval levels, credit granting limits, cash deposit procedures, and so forth. The corporatewide controls should include the following among others.

Capital Expenditure Approval Limits. Management approvals should be required for certain types of expenditures and at certain monetary limits. Dollar approval limits can vary depending on the level of management. For instance, the approval of the parent company's president may be necessary for expenditures in excess of $500,000; for amounts up to $500,000, the affiliate president. A division controller may have a dollar limit of $10,000. Further, lease commitments with total payments in excess of certain dollar limits should also require approval.

Employee Loans. Employee loans should have appropriate internal controls. These controls should have the following:

1. The various reasons that management may find appropriate to loan funds to company employees.
2. The company philosophy concerning the charging of interest on employee loans.
3. The length and method of repayment.
4. Conditions of repayment if the employee terminates his or her employment with the company.
5. A description of the proper documents acknowledging the terms and conditions of the loan, and the company officials' signatures required.

Debt/Borrowing Limits. The borrowing limits of a division or affiliate might require approval of parent company management. Once these limits have been established, the division or affiliate may make a future request that its borrowing limit be increased. The action should be justified in writing and submitted for approval.

PLANNING

Annual Budgets and Forecasts

Every organization, whether business or nonbusiness, has certain objectives. These objectives or goals usually take the form of profit or social responsibility. To achieve the objectives of the firm, it should operate efficiently. Formalized plans or budgets are important to being efficient and to achieving objectives.

During the integration period of an acquisition, the budgeting process takes on a greater sense of importance. This is because the uncertainties surrounding the future results of an acquisition are greater than the base business. Also, this is the period when the acquired company is learning a new set of procedures and must be fully acclimated into the corporation and guided toward the organization goals. Further, the preacquisition forecasts must be modified on the basis of the greater information available now that the acquisition has taken place.

Each organization has its own budgeting and forecasting procedures. The next several sections describe the type of requirements a newly acquired affiliate should expect to encounter.

Budgets and forecast should include all pertinent items of the income statement and balance sheet as delineated in the parent's procedures. The income statement obviously must include sales and income, but might include cost of goods sold, marketing, other operating expenses, interest expense/income, and taxes. The Balance Sheet should focus on current assets—primarily cash, accounts receivable, inventories, and short- or long-term debt requirements. A full balance sheet forecast may be necessary under unusual circumstances only. The frequency of financial forecasts and the other types of data required in each forecast can vary widely. An example of a forecast schedule follows:

	Data Required	
	Income Statement	Balance Sheet
Beginning of Year	Full	Full
After 1st Qtr. Actual	Full	Curr. Assets
After 2nd Qtr. Actual	Sales/IBT/Net Inc.	Curr. Assets
After 3rd Qtr. Actual	Full	Full

Long-Term Strategic Direction

The previous section dealt primarily with short-term forecasts, one to two years of financial data. The organization must be guided over the long term as well. To do this efficiently, the organization must develop a strategic direction or mission; that is, the organization must decide what role it intends to pursue and what its long-range goals are.

A long-range goal for the organization might be to become a market leader in a particular product or product group, or to increase the net profit margin by two percentage points while maintaining a 15% growth rate for sales. Therefore, long-range plans—perhaps covering 5 and 10 years—should be developed. These plans should point out how the long-range goal is to be attained. A long-range or strategic plan might be presented as follows:

1. Long-range goals with narrative describing marketing strategy, problems to be resolved, and resources needed.
2. Financial highlights, such as:

($ in thousands)	Current Year	Five-Year Plan	Ten-Year Plan
Net Trade Sales	$ 1,468	$ 2,953	$ 5,939
Net Income	$ 168	$ 396	$ 915
Net Income Margin	11.4%	13.4%	15.4%

In the previous example the goal of increasing the net profit margin may have been forecasted to be attained by becoming more efficient in production (cost of goods sold) or operating expenses. The rationale as to the areas to be improved should be identified, that is, product mix, productivity improvement, and so forth.

Long-range plans should be prepared annually and deal primarily with the income statement. It is important to look at long-range planning as a tool for management to assist the organization in achieving its goals.

Contingencies

Contingencies have been a part of the planning process since the beginning. They take the form of conservative estimates that offset the uncertainties inherent in any projection.

In financial budgeting or forecasting, contingencies take on a more formal role. They are used in forecasts to provide for those unpredictable events that might materially affect the results of operations. For example, a contingency may be an amount provided for a potential sales shortfall due to the volatility of unit sales. A contingency may also be provided for unforeseen expenses due to an abnormal situation or for discretionary projects.

Contingencies should be viewed as a planning tool, used by management in an attempt to ensure that profit objectives are achieved. That is, if a corporate goal is to achieve a net income growth of 15% over the prior year, each component of the income statement must be reviewed and a workable budget must be prepared. This budget should include conservative estimates or contingencies to offset other potential negative events if the goal is to be achieved.

Contingencies may be developed as follows:

Potential Sales Shortfall. If a sales forecast is based on a new product introduction scheduled during the year, an estimate of the potential incremental loss of profit that would result if the product was delayed should be developed based on the probability of the event happening. This amount would be the contingency.

Once a contingency has been approved as part of a forecast, it is very important that it be controlled. The danger exists that a company will expect the contingency to absorb its forecast shortfall when, in fact, it has already been committed to other uses. The responsibility for controlling the contingency lies with the chief financial officer of the division or affiliate.

Contingencies should be reported as a separate item in the budget, for example:

XYZ Company

Income Statement

	Actual	First-Year Budget	Second-Year Budget
Net Trade Sales	$ 8,500	10,000	12,000
Cost of Goods Sold	4,500	5,000	6,000
Gross Profit	4,000	5,000	6,000
Operating Expense	2,000	2,300	2,600
Contingency	—	300	600
Income Before Tax	2,000	2,400	2,800
Taxes	1,000	1,200	1,400
Net Income	$ 1,000	1,200	1,400

The uncertainty of the forecast increases in future years, so too should the contingency increase. In the example the contingency increases from 3% of sales in the first-year forecast to 5% of sales in the second-year forecast.

CHECKLIST

In a decentralized environment the acquired company will have significant autonomy and, as such, there are only a few general issues that should be given consideration.

1. Review the management structure and organization to assess the talents within the various divisions of the acquired company, particularly the financial area.
2. Develop a timetable for the orientation of the appropriate levels of management of the acquired company and arrange for visits as deemed appropriate.
3. Identify the minimum key financial data needed by parent's management to effectively monitor the acquired company's performance.
4. Identify the minimum key financial data needed for public reporting purposes by the parent and the respective due dates when this information is required.
5. Emphasize the degree of autonomy that the newly acquired company will be operating under and point out the entrepreneurial opportunities that exist.
6. Inform the management of the acquired company regarding the overall corporate goals of the parent, as well as its policies pertinent to social responsibilities.

four

EVALUATION OF ACQUIREE'S MANAGEMENT AND ACCOUNTING SYSTEMS

James Billups, CMA

CONTENTS

ACQUISITION REVIEW

Objective

The objective of the internal audit acquisition review, unlike a review of internal controls, is based on the needs of the management requesting the review. In general, it will depend on the type of acquisition being contemplated, such as acquiring the assets of a company or the technology and/or management expertise.

The types of reviews might include:

1. Analytical review of financial statements with concentration on the more significant financial areas.
2. General review of the company's accounting and reporting practices and an overview of their internal controls.
3. Verification of specific balances such as inventory, receivables, and payables. This would be used where the purchase price is as of a specific date.

Prior to commencing the review, the auditor should have a clear understanding of the objectives. The auditors' understanding of the objectives is important to the success of the review since they may be working under extreme time contraints. The final signing of the acquisition agreement may be dependent on the results of the audit work performed. This understanding will also enable the auditors to concentrate only on those areas that are important and that may have a bearing on the acquisition price, or may form the basis for adjusting the price.

Planning the Preacquisition Review

The meeting with the requestor is one of the important aspects of the planning process. The requestor should provide the auditors with information about the company, timing of the acquisition, any deadlines, financial statements, contracts, and so forth. The auditors should also take the opportunity during the meeting to determine what the requestor expects from the review and if there are any specific concerns.

1. *Information on Company.* Information obtained from the requestor should be reviewed by the auditors so that they become familiar with the company, its products, and organization. This information should provide the auditors with sufficient information to plan their review.

2. *Establish Timing of Review.* After the auditors have determined the objectives of the review and its scope, they should contact the acquiree company, preferably the chief financial officer, to arrange for a time to start the audit and indicate what information will be required when the auditors arrive on site. A timetable should be developed and discussed with the acquiree.

Audit Scope

The audit scope should be designed so that all significant areas of the company are reviewed and a determination made as to the accuracy of the financial statements in accordance with Generally Accepted Accounting Principles. While a review of internal controls is not a primary objective of the audit, the auditors should document during their review any internal control weaknesses noted and include them in the report. Follow-up audits of internal control weaknesses should be performed after the acquisition is completed.

In addition to the auditors' review of the accuracy of the company's financial information and a determination and evaluation of any potential problems, the auditors should also determine if all the requirements for the business combination have been met.

Business Combinations

The two major types of accounting for a business combination are the "purchase" or the "pooling of interests." The purchase method is when the acquiring company purchases for cash the company assets or stock; wherein, the pooling of interest method involves combining the companies by exchange of stock. The advantages and disadvantages and its tax consequences are more fully explained in Chapter 8.

The auditors' responsibility in this area is to review and determine if the criteria for the type of business combination desired have been met. The auditors should be familiar with the requirements before proceeding. If during the review, there are any questions concerning accounting for the business combination, these should be brought to the attention of management. Significant concerns could delay the final signing of the agreement until the concerns are resolved.

It is important that the auditors coordinate their audit work with others in the organization involved in the acquisition, that is, tax, insurance, personnel, legal, and so on. They should bring any concern beyond their level of expertise to the appropriate individuals in the company. However, the auditors will most likely be the individuals that company management will rely on for questions concerning the acquisition. Of all of the individuals involved in the acquisition, the auditors will probably have spent the most time with the acquiree and be more familiar with the company than others in the parent organization.

POSTACQUISITION REVIEW

Objective

Objectives of the postacquisition internal audit process are to review and evaluate the newly acquired company's internal accounting controls to determine that:

1. Transactions are properly authorized by management.
2. Transactions are properly recorded and reported to permit preparation of financial statements.
3. All assets are properly safeguarded.
4. The financial records are reliable.
5. There is compliance with management policies and procedures.

Planning the Review

Planning the review is one of the most important aspects of the examination. Because this will be the first review that is specifically directed to the acquired company's internal controls by the internal audit department, there may be very little, if any information on the company's control systems. An audit well planned prior to arrival on site will help ensure that all the acquired company's systems are effectively and efficiently reviewed. The following should be prepared by the in-charge auditor:

Audit Time Summary. Exhibit 4.1 lists the primary areas that are to be reviewed, with the budgeted time to be spent in each area. It also provides a column for the auditors to list actual time spent in the area, for variances from budget, and for the in-charge auditor to list recommendations for the

Exhibit 4.1   Audit Time Summary

Company: _____   Reviewed by: _____
Location: _____   In-Charge: _____
Audit Date/# of days: _____   Sup./Mgr.: _____
Auditors: _____

Audit Areas	Budgeted Hours	Actual Hours	Variance Over/Under Budget	Audit Budget
Accounts payable				
Accounts rec./bad debt				
Blank check/sign. plate				
Cash balances				
Cash remittances				
Petty cash				
Data center review				
Emp. rec., loans, exp.				
Fixed assets				
Income taxes				
Intercompany accounting				
Inventory/cost				
Investments				
Other B/S + P/L				
Payments cycle				
Payroll				
Production cycle				
Purchasing				

Exhibit 4.1   (Continued)

Audit Areas	Budgeted Hours	Actual Hours	Variance Over/Under Budget	Audit Budget
Revenue cycle				
Sales order/credit				
Administrative				
Analytical review				
Planning				
Plant tour & initial mtg.				
Report: on-site				
Report: Office				
Supervision				
In-depth/special requests				
Other				
Total				

Note: 1. If area is not applicable indicate by N/A.
2. If area was eliminated from planned scope or not done, identify above and explain on reverse side.
3. Significant variances between budget and actual should be explained on reverse side.

next audit. The schedule is designed to account for all time spent on the audit and to provide a basis for planning the next review of the company.

Audit Area Schedule.   Exhibit 4.2 is designed to inform the acquiree's management of the specific times that an audit area will be reviewed. It will facilitate an effective audit since management can ensure that employees will be available to answer questions and provide information to the auditors.

Exhibit 4.2   Audit Area Schedule For Local Management

Auditor

1st Week	Date: _____	Audit Area
Monday		_____
Tuesday		_____
Wednesday		_____
Thursday		_____
Friday		_____
2nd Week	Date: _____	
Monday		_____
Tuesday		_____
Wednesday		_____
Thursday		_____
Friday		_____
3rd Week	Date: _____	
Monday		_____
Tuesday		_____
Wednesday		_____
Thursday		_____
Friday		_____

Audit Program.   Develop audit programs or adopt existing programs for the areas to be reviewed.

Preaudit Staff Meeting.   The following should be discussed by the in-charge auditor with the audit staff assigned to the examination.

1. Background information about the company and the audit, for example, review of financial statements, if separately prepared.
2. Audit areas assigned to each staff person.
3. The time budget assigned to each staff person and the deadlines for the workpaper review.

This meeting will help ensure that the staff assigned has a clear understanding of the audit objective and what its responsibilities are.

Analytical Review.   If financial statements are available, an analytical review should be performed prior to visiting the company. Analytical review procedures are tests of financial information made by a study and comparison of relationships among data (usually balance sheet and statement of income figures for comparable period, quarterly and year-to-date). This will assist in determining the nature, timing, and extent of other audit procedures by identifying significant fluctuations that may require further discussion with the chief financial officer.

Management Concerns. Acquiring company concerns that are to be addressed by the auditors should be documented by the in-charge auditor on a form designed for that purpose (see Exhibit 4.3).

Documentation of the concerns will help ensure that they are addressed during the audit and the person expressing the concerns is apprised of their disposition.

Audit Approach and Scope. Preacquisition workpapers and discussions with the external auditors are excellent sources for the internal auditors to become familiar with systems of the company being acquired and can provide information that can be used to establish the scope of the audit. All significant areas of the company should be reviewed. Not only should the auditors be concerned with the company's control environment, but also its ability to conform to the acquiring company's accounting and reporting requirements.

Timing of Review. After the auditors have determined the objectives of the review and its scope, an officer of the acquired company, preferably the chief financial officer, should be contacted to arrange for a time to start the audit and to request the type of information that should be available when

Exhibit 4.3 Management Concerns
_____

Person Who Expressed Concern and Date Discussed

Nature of Concern

Disposition

| _____ | _____ |
| In-Charge | Date |
_____

the auditors arrive on site. This will save time and be less disruptive to the organization and ensure that appropriate personnel of the acquiree will be available.

In addition, a timetable should also be established with the acquired company indicating the approximate time it will take and the number of auditors that will be performing the audit. It should be clearly established prior to commencing the audit what areas the auditors will be reviewing so that all aspects of the audit are coordinated.

On Site

Initial Meeting with Chief Financial Officer. At the initial meeting with the acquired company's chief financial officer, which all auditors should attend, the following should be discussed and/or requested:

1. Discuss audit scope and provide schedule to chief financial officer indicating all the areas to be reviewed (Exhibit 4.2).
2. Request whether the acquired company management has any concerns. Any concerns should be documented (Exhibit 4.3).
3. Arrange date and time for interim and final meetings.
4. Discuss most recent financial statement and secure necessary background explanations, and so forth. The questions should have been prepared as a part of the analytical review.
5. Obtain the most recent organization chart.
6. Determine if there have been or are planned any changes in key personnel, or if there has been a rapid turnover of personnel. Recent changes in key personnel, especially in key financial areas, would be an indicator to the auditors that controls in those areas may not be operating as management intended and that there may be control weaknesses.

Financial Statement Review. If financial statements were not available during the initial planning of the audit, the financial statements should be obtained and an analytical review performed as indicated in the planning section. The results of the review should then be discussed with the chief financial officer.

Accounting Policies and Procedures. The auditors' examination in this area determines if the company's accounting policies and procedures are consistent with those of the acquiring company. In addition, the following should be determined:

1. If there have been any changes in policies and practices since the acquisition date.
2. If the accounting policies and procedures are written.
3. If they are consistently followed.
4. Who in the organization has the authority to establish them.
5. How the company ensures they are followed.
6. If they provide for the accumulation of data so that financial reports can be prepared in accordance with generally accepted accounting principles.
7. If they follow general industry practices.

If the company's accounting policies and procedures are documented and there are established procedures for revising and ensuring that they are followed, the auditors will have some assurance that there is a system in place for establishing and maintaining the company's accounting policies and procedures. If on the other hand the policies and procedures are not in written form, this could indicate that they are not regularly followed nor consistently applied from year to year. Thus, a more thorough review may be necessary. Accounting policies that the auditors may find to be inconsistent with those of the acquiring company's because of alternative accounting methods available, and which can have a significant impact on financial results, are as follows:

1. *Cost Accounting Techniques.*   This area relates to how the company costs the products it manufactures. That is, does it use standard cost, actual cost, average cost, or a hybrid method? In addition, what types of costs does the company include in its product cost?
2. *Inventory Valuation.*   This is an important area because the company's financial results could be changed significantly as a result of the valuation method used, that is, FIFO or LIFO.
3. *Depreciation Methods.*   Do book and tax depreciation differ? Do they use straight-line, sum-of-year digits, double declining balance, or other methods for book purposes?
4. *Capital Versus Expense Policy.*   What is the policy? Does it conform with the acquiring company's policies and has it been consistently followed?
5. *Investment Credit.*   What is company policy? How it is recorded?
6. *Reserves.*   Inventory, bad debts, etc. How are they determined and recorded?

The above list only indicates a few of the areas where there may be significant differences between the acquired and acquiring company's accounting procedures. Because the auditors will gain much knowledge about the company, they can be of invaluable assistance to the acquiring company by pointing out the impact on the acquired company if changes are made in the acquired company's accounting policies. However, the auditors should recognize that if the company is in an entirely different line of business than the acquiring company, the practices followed may be common for that particular industry and thus conformance to the acquiring company's policies may not be appropriate. As the policies are reviewed, this should be taken into consideration.

Accounting Systems for Transactions. A review of the acquired company's accounting transactions will not only confirm the auditors' understanding of the accounting systems but will also provide information to determine whether changes may be necessary in the systems to meet the acquiring company's accounting and reporting requirements. In reviewing the systems for transactions, the auditors should determine:

1. Number of systems for transactions.
2. How the transactions originate.
3. Who authorizes the transactions.
4. When they are approved and by whom.
5. Who reviews the transactions and when they are reviewed.
6. How the transactions are recorded—manual and/or computer.
7. Number of locations initiating and/or processing transactions and type of transactions emanating from locations.
8. If policies and procedures relating to transactions are consistently applied at all locations.
9. How information is consolidated for financial reporting.

There should be controls over all transactions regardless of where they are initiated or how they are processed. These controls should ensure that all transactions have been properly authorized, approved, and recorded.

Competence of Management. An important issue is management's familiarity with internal control concepts and concern with how the controls operate in its company. That is, does management understand the importance and objectives of internal controls? As the auditors review the company's systems, the employees who are responsible for ensuring that the systems are operating as management intended should be evaluated. Evaluation of the employees is an important aspect of the review because they are an integral part of the control system. Through observation and discussions with them about their responsibilities, the auditors will continue to expand their understanding of the systems. The auditors should determine:

1. If the company has control objectives in writing.
2. Who in the organization is primarily responsible for establishing internal control systems.
3. How management informs employees about internal controls.

Company management is one of the most important aspects of the control system because it has the responsibility to establish and maintain a system of controls that ensures transactions are properly authorized, approved, accurately recorded, and that all assets are safeguarded. It is also management's responsibility to ensure that the accounting systems are documented through flowcharts or narratives, written procedures, and employee job descriptions, and that the documentation is maintained on a current basis. If the acquiring company management can rely on the acquired company to operate an effective system of controls, integrating the company will be made that much easier.

Identification of Potential Problems.   During the auditors' review and testing of transactions, they should document their understanding of the controls in the areas reviewed and any control weaknesses noted. The auditors' workpapers should document the following:

1. The control weaknesses identified.
2. The consequences of the lack of control.
3. Any other controls that may minimize the identified weaknesses.
4. The recommendation(s) for correcting the weaknesses.

All control weaknesses or concerns should be discussed with the responsible employee in the area in order to ensure that the auditors' understanding of the system is correct and to determine if there are other controls in operations that the auditors may not be aware of. The auditors should also consider the feasibility of implementing the controls to be recommended. This is of particular importance when the company is small and resources limited. At the completion of the review, all recommendations should be discussed with the chief financial officer and agreement reached on action to be taken. The auditor should offer copies of the flowcharts and/or narratives developed in the course of the audit to the company. These can then be used to help document the company's internal control systems.

Compatibility of Systems. All systems should be reviewed to determine degree of compatibility with the acquiring company's policies and procedures and the extent of any differences. Through review of the company systems the auditors can determine the amount of effort required to integrate the company.

Report to Management

The report to management should give background information on the company and document for management the auditors' findings and recommendations for improvements in the control system.

Structure and Content. The audit report should contain:

1. A cover letter.
2. Background information.
3. Overall assessment of the company's control system.
4. Scope of review.
5. Control weakness(s) noted and recommendations for correcting.
6. Management response.

Cover Letter. The letter should be addressed to the acquiring company's chief financial officer and indicate the date and type of audit performed.

Background Information. This section should provide information about the company; among the information included should be its locations, products or services, types of accounting systems, computer systems utilized, planned changes in systems and key changes in personnel, and any other pertinent information. The auditors should include any information that would be of benefit to the reader.

Scope of Review. This section should describe the work that the auditors performed in the areas reviewed.

Conclusion. This section would contain the auditors' opinion about the company's procedures and controls. The auditors' conclusions would indicate the significance of the report. Obviously, a report with an overall inadequate conclusion will require more attention from all of the report's audiences than will a report with a conclusion that internal controls and procedures were adequate. The conclusion aids the auditors in achieving their purposes by informing management of their work and findings and by encouraging prompt remedial action to correct any inadequacies. It also helps the reader by indicating the degree of problems noted and the importance of remedial action.

Control Weaknesses Noted.   The control weaknesses identified should be described as follows:

1. The nature of the problem.
2. Consequence—describe what the effect or possible effect problem has on company.

Recommendation.   This section identifies the specific recommendations to correct the weakness.

Management Response.   Management's reactions and responses to the recommendations would be reported in this section.

Presented in Exhibit 4.4 is a portion of an audit report.

Report Distribution.   Because an audit report contains confidential information, the distribution of the report should be determined by corporate management.

Postaudit Follow-Up.   The auditors should ensure that all recommendations made and agreed to are implemented. Frequently, recommendations made cannot be implemented immediately but must be done over a period of time. As a result of the audit and the other changes needed to adapt the accounting and control systems and procedures to the requirements of the acquiring company, changes in responsibilities will likely be required. Also, other parts of the acquired company could be affected by the changes. Thus, many recommendations may not be implemented immediately. The auditors should continue to follow up with the company until the recommendations are satisfactorily implemented. The auditors' follow-up and the response from the company should be documented.

Implementation Assistance of Company Accounting Policies.   The auditors should not only look at their role as reviewers and evaluators of the company's internal control systems but also as consultants to the new management. The auditors' knowledge of the acquiring company's accounting policies and

Exhibit 4.4   Audit Report

XYZ Company, Inc.
(July 19XX)

Introduction

The XYZ Company was acquired in February 19XX. It manufactures and sells various consumer products. Its main office, manufacturing facility, and warehouses are located in Akron, Ohio. All of the company's financial systems are computerized. This audit was our first review of the company.

Conclusion

Based on our review, we consider the company's system of internal accounting controls and procedures to be inadequate.

The implementation of the recommendations included in this report will significantly improve the company's controls and procedures in the areas reviewed. However, because our review was limited in scope, it is likely that this report does not include all recommendations that would result from a more comprehensive audit of the areas reviewed.

Scope

This was our first review of the company since the acquisition. Our review was performed at the request of corporate management. The purpose of the review was to identify any control weaknesses which exist in the company's internal accounting controls and procedures. Our review was also intended to provide information and to enable management to ensure that there are no weaknesses included in any planned changes in existing controls and procedures.

Summary of Recommendations

Recommendation	Management Response
I. *General*	
Recommended that:	
A. Subsidiary records be reconciled to the general ledger at least quarterly.	Will implement
B. Invoices paid, petty cash slips, expense reports, and all supporting documentation be canceled under the direction of the check signer or approver.	Will implement
C. Effective input/output controls be developed and utilized in the processing of inventory and accounts payable transactions.	Will implement
D. 1. The custody of the petty cash fund be transferred to an independent individual.	Will implement

Exhibit 4.4   (Continued)

Recommendation	*Management Response*
2. All miscellaneous cash receipts be delivered directly to an independent person and that a control listing be prepared and subsequently compared to the bank deposit.	Will implement
II. *Inventory Cost* Recommended that: A. Alternative inventory/cost systems be promptly evaluated and that a suitable system be developed.	Management intends to implement a new inventory/cost system, and is presently investigating manufacturing resources planning (MRP) procedures.
III. *Accounts Payable* Recommended that: A. The vendor master file be reviewed periodically by company management.	Will implement
B. Only approved purchase orders containing appropriate prices be accepted as approval to pay vendor invoices.	Will implement
C. All open receiving reports be reviewed at quarter-end and accruals be recorded if the amounts are material.	Will implement
Sales Order/Credit Recommended that: A. The accuracy of the sales cutoff be reviewed at the end of each quarter and that all significant adjustments be recorded.	Will implement
B. A monthly report summarizing all credit memos by amount and category be prepared for the review and approval of management.	Will implement

procedures can be a source that the acquired company can use for assistance in the following ways:

1. Acting as a "sounding board" for questions.

2. Reviewing new systems before they are implemented to ensure controls are addressed in the new systems.

3. Helping to get an adequate control environment in place by emphasizing to management that internal control is a management tool.

4. Familiarize management with the acquiring company's policies and procedures, that is, applying and interpreting procedures.
5. Find problems before systems are formulated.
6. Emphasizing to the acquiring company's management the difficulties the company may have in meeting the acquiring company's requirements because of size, number of locations, limited staff, or other problems.

Accounting Policies. Because the policies and procedures of large and complex companies can be voluminous and can cover a broad range of topics, the auditors can be invaluable to both the acquired and acquiring company in assisting them in their efforts to integrate the company.

CHECKLIST

Acquisition Review

1. Inventory.
    (a) Excess and obsolete.
    (b) Valuation.
    (c) Breakdown of raw material, work-in-process, and finished goods inventories.
2. Accounts receivable.
    (a) Types of customers—distributors, direct sales, and so on.
    (b) Bad debt allowance reserve provision—is it sufficient?
3. Purchase commitments.
    (a) Written contracts.
    (b) Company liability, if canceled.
4. Product warranty liability.
5. Pension liability.
6. Accrued liabilities for litigation.
7. Unaudited federal, state, and local taxes, years and exposure.
8. Leases—extent of and how accounted for.
9. Unrecorded liabilities.
10. Provision for "discontinued businesses."
11. Is R&D consistent with Financial Accounting Standard 2?
12. Goodwill.

13. Breakdown of domestic/international business.
14. Expense and capitalization policies.
15. Age of plant and equipment.
16. Tax and book depreciation differences.
17. Competence of management.
18. Key management personnel.

Post Acquisition Review

1. Evaluation of internal control system.
2. Management awareness of internal controls.
3. Accounting policies and procedures.
4. Security over assets.
5. Timing of sales reconciliation.
6. Inventory and bad debt reserves.
7. Depreciation methods.
8. Number of accounting systems for transactions.
9. Compatibility of business operations.
10. Impact, if company changes to acquired company accounting policies.
11. Integration of company—how difficult?

five

AN ACQUIREE'S VIEWPOINT
Problems, Concerns, Coping with the Changes

David C. Boehm, MBA, CMA, CPA

CONTENTS

INITIAL STAGES

Understanding the Acquiree

The task of integrating the accounting and reporting systems of acquired companies will fall to the management accountant. That person would be wise to develop an understanding of what the prevailing feelings and overall business climate are likely to be from the viewpoint of the acquiree's personnel, especially the staff of the finance area.

Just as endeavoring to develop standard costs with no knowledge of cost accounting concepts appears foolish, so would attempting to integrate the acquiree without an appreciation of its organization's problems and concerns caused by the acquisition.

More often than not, the acquiree will be a significantly smaller company in terms of sales, assets, and number of employees. Although there are exceptions, this assumption is followed in this chapter. In addition, because it is the *centralized approach* that would generate the greatest amount of change for the acquiree, most of the chapter is written assuming that the acquiree must perform in that operational mode.

The Acquiree's Hopes and Fears

If the acquiree had been in financial trouble or if internal conflicts existed prior to the merge, the acquiree's management team and its employees may very well have been looking forward to wholesale changes that would inject new life into the entity. This situation would lead one to expect that the acquiring company's management would be greeted as saviors. However, even if this was the case, the existing euphoria would dissipate rapidly after reality takes hold.

Once the news has reached the personnel of the acquiree, whether it be through a leak and then ground up via the rumor mill or through a prepared, formal announcement, there undoubtedly will be some employees with expectations such as:

1. Now the company will have funding for *my* project.
2. There will finally be some management changes making *my* job better.

3. The future will be rosier and *I* will feel more secure.
4. *My* benefits will increase and pay scales will be revised upward.
5. *I'll* finally have a chance to display my skills.
6. There will be some opportunities for *me*.
7. *Our* systems will become more sophisticated.
8. *I* will enjoy being in a learning mode.
9. Internal conflicts will abate and *my* working conditions will improve.
10. The larger company will provide enjoyable perks for *me*.

Conversely, there are usually even greater numbers of employees who will either initially (because of distorted communications) or eventually (because of the change) share the following heartfelt concerns:

1. The new management will eliminate *my* project; I will be terminated.
2. *I* will have to answer to "one of them."
3. They will close the plant and move the operations to their state; *I* will have to relocate or lose my job.
4. *My* pay and benefits will be cut.
5. *I'll* have to prove myself all over again.
6. *I* will not have any chance to advance because *I* am an XYZ manager not someone from ABC.
7. *My* freedom will be eliminated through the red tape and bureaucracy.
8. *I* will be told what to do even though they don't know our business.
9. *Our* close-knit small "family" will be broken up.
10. *I* will lose my title, my office, my perks.

While in this "news stage," the hopes and fears (especially the latter) can cause the following phenomena at the operations of the acquiree:

1. Morale can be affected unfavorably (largely by unfounded fears or worst-case projections).
2. Productivity can be affected.
3. Employees may be commiserating with each other during work hours, thus causing further impacts on the above-mentioned points.
4. The health of certain employees (especially middle management types) can be affected.
5. Nerves may be on edge as tension builds.

6. All communications may be accepted "with a grain of salt."
7. Management may become uncertain as to how to operate the company in anticipation of receiving instructions from the new owners.
8. Employees may begin to sense the concern of their management and start to develop further concerns.
9. Employees may feel abandoned and, in the case of known monetary gains achieved by the former principals, a feeling of resentment sets in.
10. The employees may sense that the operation is out of control, their future is in jeopardy, and there is no one to turn to for help.

The Inevitable Confusion

"Finally" the management of the acquiring company begins to communicate with the acquiree . . . do they ever! Phone calls, visits, written memos, desired procedures, mandated deadlines, different policies, new benefits, and seemingly thousands of other changes.

Reporting relationships are established (worse if they are not), the ground rules for obtaining approvals are created and objectives are developed. There has surely been a disruption of the flow of the business and confusion reigns supreme.

Thankfully, the "news stage" is short-lived, and the management of the acquiring company begins to understand the enormity of its task and starts to realize that the acquiree is "different" and that many months of hard work lie ahead if the merger is to be a success.

Formulation of Opinions

Employees of the acquiree begin to form opinions of what their future holds by the acquiring company's style and apparent philosophy by judging the initial visitors. Nothing goes unnoticed as offices and shops alike begin to buzz with observations on:

1. Dress (three-piece suits or sport jackets?)
2. Grooming (short hair look-alikes or the latest styles?)
3. Age (fresh MBA grads or 40-year veterans?)
4. Habits (cigar smokers or health food advocates?)
5. Priorities (production or a multicolored company newsletter?)
6. Emphasis (experience or stressing education?)

7. Values (new wooden desks or used metal furniture from an auction?)

8. Image (arrived via a Lincoln limousine or drove their own Rent-a-Wreck?)

9. Language (walking Thesaurus or words that would embarrass a sailor?)

10. Style (two-hour lunch at the city's finest French restaurant or a quick bite with the employees in the lunch room?)

11. Hours (knocked off early to check out the local links or worked into the night?)

12. Patience (upset at the slightest concern or carefully explained their requests?)

13. Warmth (spoke only to the highest individuals in management or shook hands with everyone including the boiler operator?)

14. Approach (dictated immediate changes or asked questions for the purpose of learning the operation?)

15. Knowledge (did not know which end was up or offered viable suggestions?)

16. Planning (seemed wishy-washy or came across as having firm convictions based on a well-thought-out study?)

Although some of the aforementioned items are merely ingredients to keep conversations spiced, others will hamper the integration process with needless delays caused by a lack of understanding of each other's role and background. Signals that are magnified become major obstacles to building a rapport and fostering needed communication between the two organizations.

As contact is increased between the two groups, defenses are relaxed and the acquiree begins to formulate its projection of the future as the acquiring company's priorities unfold.

PITFALLS OF THE INTEGRATION PROCESS

"Nothing's Going to Change"

The onset of the integration process promises to produce many frustrations through faulty communications and overall misunderstandings of the acquiring company's actions and the acquiree's reactions. In an effort to calm down the acquiree's president (general manager) and in an attempt to quell that individual's mounting fears, some high-level manager in a position of authority and responsibility with respect to the acquiree is likely to utter that famous line: "Don't worry, nothing is going to change," followed by "You will still be in charge and your authority and autonomy will not be affected." What ridiculous statements! Of course there will be changes; *there have already been changes*—the process of having to undergo an integration process because of the merger certainly wasn't on the acquiree's agenda a few short months ago!

Unfortunately, those are the words that the president (general manager) wanted to hear; now subordinates' fears can be allayed by disseminating that same message downward through the organization. Those words can be likened to the "vote of confidence" that a baseball manager receives from the front office on occasion. This false assurance, however, may have a calming effect on the acquiree's management for some short time span and then a storm should be expected.

At some point the acquiree may observe (or imagine) many of the following happenings (changes) affecting the organization:

1. Someone in "headquarters" approves actions and expenditures that once were carried out locally.

2. Duties have changed and certain functions have been transferred to headquarters.

3. Disappearances of the old company name, logo, and familiar green and purple sign.

4. What once was a proud company may now be called a division, subsidiary, plant, or simply a product line—the outpost effect.

5. A new organization and complete revamping of titles (the former V.P. finance may now be called the plant controller).

6. A loss of pay may be sustained by many employees and management types alike so as to "ensure compatibility and fairness" with the pay scales of the acquiring company.

7. Constant telephone calls and abrupt visits.

8. A complete new chart of accounts that the accounting area is fumbling with.

9. A loss of many employees due to voluntary resignations brought about by frustrations and by induced terminations due to incompatibility or duplication of overhead.

10. A 4000-page procedures book.

11. New reports that do anything but fairly represent the activities of the acquiree.

12. New buzz words, acronyms, and pet expressions.

13. Overhead charges from headquarters for "services rendered."

14. That constant line about ". . . the way we do it at ABC . . ." and the promises about . . . "how much better things are going to be . . ."

15. A feeling of being treated like a second-class citizen.

16. Difficulty in getting ideas communicated upward.

17. A coldness that has set in.

The Acquiree Looks Up and Sees . . .

The acquiring company's desire to revamp the place in its own image becomes evident as management communicates its priorities and desires, which may include:

1. An image enhancement

    (a) Sprucing up the acquiree's facilities with expensive cleaning services, fresh coats of paint, a load of sod, shrubs, and some plants for the lobby.

    (b) Elimination of the vending machines and construction of a cafeteria rivaling that French restaurant down the street.

    (c) Printing of elaborate employee handbooks to provide everyone with a working knowledge of their rights and benefits.

    (d) Scrapping of existing furniture and purchasing modern desks, chairs, and credenzas for all office workers.

    (e) Junking the company's 1959 Edsel station wagon and replacing it with a new air-conditioned van complete with stereo.

    (f) Dropping the brand-X telephone system and installing a modern system that enables the user to call-forward messages, page, and eliminate the need to remember phone numbers.

2. Required written reports on:

    (a) Short-term forecasts

    (b) Sales and production

    (c) Employee head count and turnover

    (d) Affirmative Action

    (e) Monthly activities

    (f) United Way and U.S. Savings Bond participation

    (g) Contributions to charity and community organizations

    (h) Five-year management succession plan

    (i) Ten-year long-range plan

3. Creation of new positions:
   (a) Telephone Coordinator
   (b) Editor of the Employee Newsletter
   (c) Director of Office Furniture
   (d) Auto Fleet Coordinator
   (e) Financial Analyst
   (f) Manager of Employee Relations
4. Mandated meetings for
   (a) Safety
   (b) The Chairman of the Board's upcoming visit
   (c) The company picnic
   (d) Articles for the company's newsletter

Obviously, the size and business maturity of the acquiree will play a major part in determining the applicability of the above lists. The important issue is that there is a much greater chance of the smaller company's previous priorities being focused on production, plus sales and profits, rather than on the looks of the facilities, status in the community, or long-range forecasting.

The Tendency To Act Superior

If the acquiree is relatively young (in business years) and smaller than the acquiror, there is a greater chance that the newly acquired entity could be described as possessing entrepreneurial spirit, having concern over pennies, and being run like the proverbial ma and pa corner grocery store. In all likelihood everyone knows everyone else by their first name, procedures are either verbal or if written, rarely followed, information systems and office automation are nonexistent or rudimentary, and control is present thanks mainly to the strong rule of the company's founder or current CEO. The small company generally has a disdain for formal meetings, viewing them as entirely nonproductive—the company operates on short phone calls, quick impromptu meetings, and an informal day-to-day style that allows anything and everything to be expedited. By necessity, people are hired, materials are purchased, supplies are obtained, products are manufactured, and goods are shipped and if some policies and procedures are followed along the way, so much the better.

In addition, because a small operation generally does not have the funding available to train and develop experts in narrow fields, most of the acquiree's management will be "jack-of-all-trades types" although masters of none. This may lead the acquiring company to conclude (erroneously) that the acquiree's people are inexperienced, unskilled, and poorly educated.

A key item that should be kept at the mental forefront is that the acquiree does know its business. In fact, if the acquiring company is a conglomerate and the latest acquisition represents a plunge into a new product line or new market, the acquiree knows its business better than the acquiring company. One way to look at the current situation is that the acquiree was intelligent and shrewd enough to become associated with you! It makes no sense to tell the acquiree how to run its operation or set priorities or make major decisions impacting the acquiree until the acquiring company's management learns the new business. Once a working knowledge of the new operation is obtained, the goal should be that of participation, not dictation.

INCREASING THE ODDS FOR SUCCESS

Impact on Finance

Of all the divisions (manufacturing, marketing, personnel, etc.) likely to exist in most organizations, the one that may incur the greatest number and most dramatic changes is the finance division. In support of this contention, the following list is offered:

1. The finance division (controller, managers, accountants) is considered administrative overhead to begin with, and the acquiring company probably has a complete duplication of the entire list of positions.
2. Economies of scale should eliminate specialized functions at the acquiree's site via centralization at headquarters. (Among these functions are payroll, taxes, credit and accounts receivable, and cash management. Other candidates might be fixed-asset accounting and forecasting.)
3. If the acquiree is to be operated as a plant location, the areas of accounts payable, financial reporting (general accounting), and financial analysis (project accounting) may also fall victim to efficiency, leaving essentially a cost accounting department behind.
4. The acquiree's chart of accounts will almost assuredly be revamped.
5. Deadlines may be accelerated.
6. One-way requests usually start flowing from headquarters.

7. If the acquiree had no (few) mechanized systems, the introduction to full-blown EDP could be mind-boggling.
8. New policies and procedures along with new report formats will probably be imposed.

If problems are to be solved, surprises avoided, and anxieties minimized, the design of a careful well-thought-out plan would be desirable. The strategy should have as its central theme the human element, since if the accounting integration process is going to be successful, it will be because people cooperated with and understood each other.

Acquiree's Head of Finance

The first task that should be accomplished is to envision what the acquiree's financial functions and organizational structure should be a year from now and determine those events that would assure success. Included in this initial process should be a decision on who should be the head of that finance department. The least disruptive to the acquiree would be to allow the current head to continue in the role and plan the organization accordingly. The least desirable (but probably most often used) alternative is to select some charger type from headquarters and have the individual storm into the acquiree's camp. Although this would appear to be something extremely beneficial to wrapping up the integration process in the fastest way, there are many unfavorable ramifications of this alternative that would seriously impede progress. Prominent among these are:

1. The action could be interpreted as a sign that the acquiring company is comprised of hatchet types who may begin to bring more managers from headquarters, filling key slots without regard to the talents of the acquiree's management.
2. The new head of finance will be a "lion in the leopard's den" and could be treated as an outsider by both subordinates and local management peers.
3. There's an excellent chance that other valued finance employees would "jump ship" before giving the new captain a chance.

Obviously, this decision must be made in concert with the acquiree's local management and the individual in the acquiring company's senior management who has been charged with the operational responsibility of the acquiree.

Integration Coordinator Concept

Assuming that the decision on the head of finance has been made (either the incumbent stays or an outsider comes in), the next step is for the finance management of the acquiring company to take a bold leap and plunge deeply into the integration process and appoint an experienced, well-rounded intelligent management accountant who would be vested with the assignment of ensuring the success of the financial integration. This individual should possess the following:

1. A solid history of achievements.
2. Exceptional interpersonal skills with demonstrated sensitivity to human needs.
3. The ability to devise imaginative solutions quickly.

This "integration coordinator" will take on the following role:

1. The position's home office will remain at headquarters, although an unlimited amount of time would be spent at the acquiree's facility.
2. The individual would act in the capacity of friend, advisor, and liaison to the acquiree's financial division *and would have no other routine duties.*
3. The position would report to the acquiring company's chief financial officer but have dotted-line responsibility to the head of finance at the acquiree.
4. The integration coordinator would be at the disposal of the acquiree's financial management and would:
   (a) Help resolve conflicts.
   (b) Ensure that any snags impeding progress are removed.
   (c) Act as interpreter for both parties.
   (d) Recommend changes and have the necessary authority for implementation.
   (e) Prepare weekly reports to both the management of the acquiree and the acquiring company on the progress of the integration.

During the postmerger period many surprises are likely to surface, and certainly the president of the acquiring company may react to the recommendation of an integration coordinator as an expensive shock ($50,000 to $75,000). It may be worthwhile to recall some of the words of a popular commercial that advises the American public that "You can pay me now or . . ." The integration process can be tedious and bumpy—the integration coordinator provides cheap insurance and could be the equivalent of a quality investment.

Reporting Relationships

Even if the eventual goal is to create a financial organization that includes a partial matrix organization, it would be wise to avoid taking any action in pursuit of that goal during the integration process. The heretofore recommended steps (decide on the financial head and establish the integration coordinator position) have been made in an attempt to eliminate confusion and establish a clear-cut pattern of leadership. The financial management of the acquiree must understand who to take direction from. In a matrix organization, some of that individual's functions will be split, leading to further bewilderment. If financial representation is the issue, a good rule of thumb would be to provide the financial resources to support the function locally unless the function (e.g., marketing and/or research) is being transferred. This recommendation is consistent with the theme to make as few changes as possible. Furthermore, remote financial representation at headquarters that duplicates activities that continue to be provided by the acquiree seems to be an unnecessary change.

Measuring Profitability

The next decision that must be made sounds financial in nature, but in reality is an emotional one that has far-reaching humanistic ramifications—integrating the acquiree into the fold via "the books." Depending on which profitability measurement is chosen, it could breed another round of confusion and resentment.

Separate Division. From the perspective of the acquiree the least disruptive and most rewarding alternative for measuring profitability is to treat the acquiree as a division for income statement reporting purposes. As discussed earlier, certain accounting functions will probably be transferred for reasons of efficiency and thus the balance sheet will not remain intact, but the P&L is the statement that generates the most concern. It is the "report card" that measures the acquiree and is constantly and closely watched.

If the merger involved a vertical integration of a supplier, it would be ideal if the issue of transfer pricing could be postponed for a year as this debate is counterproductive and has no impact on bottom-line profits of the corporation.

The major reasons for these recommendations are the following:

1. Although report formats may be slightly altered, major closing procedures generally remain unchanged.
2. The acquiree's accounting staff should derive a certain feeling of comfort in preparing schedules they are familiar with.
3. There is usually a certain amount of pride displayed in presenting the financial results of the operation, especially if it had been a profitable entity before the merger.

Unique Product Line. If the separate division suggestion is not feasible, the second choice of the acquiree would be that of product line measurement (quasi-division approach), especially if the acquiring company has plans of overhauling the place with many corporate frills. This approach would require an identification of all revenues and costs associated with the products of the acquiree without regard to source or location. This suggestion represents a workable compromise for the following reasons:

1. Only minor changes to the closing procedures are necessary.
2. The acquiree may have generated studies in the past that were essentially product line income statements and thus may be familiar with the concepts.
3. The acquiree has an incentive to properly identify and understand the costs attributable to its product line.
4. The resulting reports provide a nonthreatening analysis that will help alleviate the "we-they problem" since the acquiree's company has been dissolved for internal reporting purposes.
5. The acquiree has something tangible with which to identify and although it represents a definite change, there is still a thread of commonality with the prior operation.

Plant Location. The alternative least desirable in the eyes of the acquiree is that of destroying the old company's image, completely swallowing up its product lines and communicating to the employees of the acquiree that they are now working at one of the "plant locations" of the acquiring company. Among the reasons that this proves to be the most distasteful of the alternatives include:

1. Significant changes in functions, responsibilities, policies, procedures, and staffing must occur in order to work in a plant location mode as opposed to operating as a separate division.

2. The true meaning of headquarters versus an outpost will manifest itself into feelings of being treated as second-class citizens.
3. The acquiree has lost all that is familiar to it.
4. There will be no question that someone else is running "our company"—a complete loss of operational control.

RECOMMENDATIONS

Achieving Goal Congruence

Even if the acquiring company moves slowly and acts cautiously, it will be extremely difficult for the acquiree to shake itself of the feeling that "a stranger is trying to tell us what to do" or the sensation that "they don't know our problems and concerns."

Before priorities can be assigned and deadlines can be established, the acquiring company should develop a strategy that has as its key element a goal to prevent the disruption of the work flow (day-to-day business operation) of the acquiree. Only under these (general) circumstances can the acquiring company expect to receive a "buy-in" of its intended goals and objectives of the integration process.

Many pitfalls can be easily avoided with a well-thought-out plan that concentrates on the human element and that is quickly communicated to the employees of the acquiree. Included in the communications should be an admission by the acquiring company that there will, by necessity, be some changes—some that will be noticed immediately, others that will evolve over the next year, and still others that will be subtle, gradual, or unforeseen at present but looking back two years from now will definitely have occurred. Some nonthreatening examples of each type should be offered along with a commitment to keep informing the acquiree's employees of expected changes. Employees understand that a company is in business to provide profits for its shareholders and do not expect to be showered with unearned gifts, benefits, and compensation. They do expect to be treated fairly and honestly. They can cope with news that appraises them of changes, even if it affects them negatively. What is completely unnerving, however, is no communications whatsoever and then bombshells.

Suggestions for the Acquiring Company

1. Develop a strategy for the integration process with a realistic timetable, remembering that the process will be fraught with surprises, roadblocks, delays, resistance, and confusion.

2. Decide on the long-term structure of the acquiree's finance department and, if necessary, overstaff initially. There will undoubtedly be some turnover and the fact that additional resources have been provided may be viewed as a favorable harbinger of things to come.

3. Try to retain the services of the acquiree's existing head of finance and appoint the integration coordinator ASAP! Yes, do it, even though it appears to cost money.

4. Insist that no visits be allowed to the acquiree unless approved in advance by the integration coordinator and the head of finance at the acquiree. A written request should be prepared stating the objectives of the trip. Demand a trip report from everyone visiting the acquiree. (This is especially critical if the acquiring company's headquarters are located in the Northeast and the acquiree's facilities are in Southern California and the integration process has commenced in mid-winter.)

5. There is no doubt that an enormous amount of time, energy, and money will be expended during the acquisition process. It is extremely foolish to waste those resources by acting in haste and bungling the integration process. If there is one thing that's on the side of both the acquiring company and the acquiree, it is time. Patience should be the watchword.

6. Once management is convinced that a sound plan has been developed, act swiftly. Make as many personnel changes as are reasonable and practical (plus any other major changes deemed crucial), announce the moves and communicate to the acquiree that, barring significant unfavorable conditions, the new structure will be in place "for quite some time." Although this may seem to contradict point 5, it is instead an integral aspect of points 1 and 5. These initial steps of the integration process can be summarized as follows:

   (a) Proceed deliberately in the beginning.

   (b) Develop a sound, logical plan.

   (c) When the time comes to act, move quickly and make necessary changes.

   (d) Keep your word and give the new organizational structure the latitude it needs to achieve the desired objectives.

7. After the required changes have been announced, patience again comes into play, along with optimism and confidence that the new organization will be successful in reaching agreed-upon goals.

8. Meet with the newly defined team. Work together to construct an overall game plan encompassing the objectives that the acquiree is

expected to meet over the next year. Establish clearly defined check-points. Provide enthusiasm and encouragement to the acquiree's management as they work toward those objectives.

9. Be aware that there will be setbacks. Although no one likes to be the recipient of an unsatisfactory review, it is extremely important for the acquiree's management to know where they stand. Hence, the acquiring company has the delicate responsibility to discuss and help correct those aspects that are not consistent with the agreed-upon plan. It is openness, firmness, and consistency that will get the job done, not the all too often perceived easier path of temporarily ignoring problems, soft-pedaling issues, and reacting needlessly to small issues.

10. If the acquired business is one in which the acquiring company's management has little or no expertise, it would be wise to tread lightly until experience provides the business acumen necessary to properly manage the new operation.

11. Although it is the acquiring company's managers who are in "power," it doesn't necessarily mean that they are better than *all* of the managers who are employed by the acquiree. Although the newly acquired personnel may have worked for a different company, they may have been in a different business and they may look at things from a completely different perspective. However, different is not synonymous with incapable.

12. The single most important detail that will permeate a successful integration process is that of good communication. The most carefully thought-out plans, most creative ideas, and the best intentions will all be wasted without it.

Suggestions for the Acquiree's Management

1. Despite how well or how poorly the integration process is proceeding, the acquiree's management still has a responsibility to its subordinates. In that light they must be supportive of the new postmerger combined corporation and project an attitude of confidence and demonstrate those same leadership traits that were present prior to the merger. Even if their own future is cloudy, complaining or wearing their own feelings on their sleeves will not benefit them or their subordinates, plus it will serve to undermine the integration process.

2. Attempt to understand how the acquiring company intends to run the operation and try to discover how the acquiree's management team fits in.

3. Project an attitude of cooperation. This has some favorable (individual) possible results and few, if any, negative ones, for example:

   (a) It may impress the new management team.

   (b) It should accelerate a successful completion of the integration process.

   (c) It could encourage a spirit of teamwork, thereby sparking the attitude of subordinates.

   (d) It may generate a spirit of teamwork that could lead the subordinates into sensing that their work lives are falling into place again with management leading them in a specific direction.

4. Level with subordinates on the entire issue of change and let them know that there will indeed be some changes including many that may leave them in better shape than if the merger had not taken place. Generate discussion on issues like:

   (a) The fact that it makes economic sense to centralize some functions and have them performed at headquarters.

   (b) That management of the acquiring company has been charged with the responsibility of the operation of the acquiree and hence may make decisions that may be locally unpopular but may in fact be wise in the long-term and beneficial to the corporation as a whole.

   (c) If the operation was once a separate company, and is now but a division or a plant location of the acquiring company, provide honest examples of the projected effects of being an "outpost," including the fact that extremely important local issues may not be a priority item at all to headquarters.

   (d) It would be realistic to assume that if procedural and reporting differences exist, it will be up to the acquiree to change in order to satisfy the needs of the acquiring company.

   (e) The fact that, especially in the beginning, there will be a flurry of questions and requests from headquarters on virtually everything.

   (f) That there's an excellent probability (especially if the acquiree is relatively small) that computerized systems will be introduced, thus changing forever the mechanics of many job functions. It would also be wise to point out that rarely do these systems eliminate jobs (in total) and that the change represents an opportunity for all concerned.

   (g) The fact that every company has its own personality, philosophies, and management styles but just as everyone working at the acquiree's place of business was able to adapt to its peculiarities, with time everyone will adjust to the new company's ways.

Suggestions for Both

One attitude that the management of both the acquiring company and the acquiree should strive to eliminate as rapidly as possible is the "we–they" attitude that emerges in all business combinations. Unless both management teams develop a sense of awareness for this problem, the integration process will be extended unnecessarily. Each time someone at headquarters talks about "those ding-a-lings" at Acquireeville or conversely "those pompous yo-yo's at Acquiring Heights," steps in the wrong direction have taken place. Although time will alter those opinions slightly, each management team must actively eliminate those attitudes with their own display of cooperation and respect for each other.

One way to start eliminating "we–they-isms" is to hold meetings with representatives of like functions (e.g., a conference on MRP with individuals from the acquiring company's materials management and cost accounting departments along with the same areas of the acquiree). Further, holding these meetings on a rotating basis at headquarters, at the acquiree's facility, and then at (neutral) remote sites will further help to strengthen a bond between the groups as they develop common goals and view each other as resources and allies, not enemies. The effect on the success of the entire process that socializing after work has should not be underestimated.

It was inferred earlier that the fewer the internal personnel changes the better; but as the merger nears the end of its first year, corporate management should be seeking to rotate middle management types from headquarters to the acquiree and vice versa. Although each one will initially be treated as an outsider (especially the transferee from headquarters), the benefits to the individuals involved, to the corporation as a whole, to the management teams at both locations, and specifically to the integration process itself are enormous. The individuals involved will develop a sense of awareness of the "other guy's" problems and in particular to the ongoing dilemma caused by any uncooperating individual of each one's former business residence. Each transferee will begin to feel an allegiance toward both parties and thus become instrumental in fostering required communication between the groups.

One of the sorest and most misunderstood points in a business combination is the problem-causing accounting issue of "allocations from headquarters." While senior management and accountants alike relish the idea of meaningful product line income statements and divisional P&Ls, it is not necessary for all fixed costs to have homes on these reports. In addition, although it is generally desirable for operations management of profit centers to "understand" that they must carry "their fair share" of corporate overhead, communicating the "equitable" charges may serve to create a tidal wave of emotionalism that is rivaled only when the next accounting period rolls around and the arguments start anew. There is nothing wrong per se with corporate allocations or with preparing product line income statements and divisional P&Ls but there is also no reason that the management team has to be made aware of the paper entries that are prepared so as to apportion all corporate overhead expenses. Despite clear and consistent logic on the reasons behind an allocation of this nature, the acquiree's management team will view the procedure as an excuse for the acquiring company to eliminate its expense problems by using the acquiree's books as a dumping ground. Another facet of the issue is that of "charges for services rendered," which elevates the acquiree's outrage to new heights. Rarely is the acquiree convinced that the charges are necessary or fair. Worse, no one asked for the services to be provided in the first place.

Rather than entering the arena to begin with, the recommendation is to develop the allocations at a very senior level of management at headquarters and communicate to the acquiree the resulting effects of the allocations in product line income statement format. Since the acquiree cannot control these charges, it cannot be held accountable for the effect that these charges have on the score card. The real issue may be that the acquiree is not meeting desired profits, but that message can be communicated without ever discussing corporate allocations. In any case, even if someone is determined to be in the allocations business, why do it now? Time is still an ally and the integration process does not need to be derailed for any nonproductive, emotional reasons.

CHECKLIST

1. Obtain reports of the acquiree's historical financial data.
2. Acquire knowledge of why the merger took place.
3. Become familiar with the acquiree's present organization, products, problems, and so on.
4. Understand the preintegration business (emotional) climate.
5. Develop an insight into the plan and strategies for the integration process.
6. Infuse realism into priorities, deadlines, and key milestones.

7. Decide on the acquiree's financial head and long-term organizational structure.
8. Appoint an integration coordinator.
9. Enforce the trip report requirement.
10. Open up communications on expected changes.
11. Treat the acquiree's employees as equals.
12. Delay nonessential procedural and format changes.
13. Disdain the "corporate allocation for services rendered" concept.
14. Avoid the "we at headquarters do it this way" syndrome.
15. Listen to the ideas of the acquiree's staff members.
16. Accept the premise that time is an ally.
17. Generate enthusiasm and demonstrate a genuine desire to work together during the integration process.

six

SPECIAL CONSIDERATIONS FOR INTERNATIONAL ACQUISITIONS

Tarun K. Bhatia, MBA, CMA, CPA

CONTENTS

INTRODUCTION

During the twentieth century the world has gone through tremendous change. This change has been apparent in every aspect of life. One of the important changes, which expanded in the post–World War II era, has been the "internationalization" of companies. It is quite apparent now that the world has shrunk in many ways, especially in the business arena. Various developments in communication, transportation, and other fields have made this all the easier. Global economic activity involving production, distribution, warehousing, marketing, and sales to varying degrees is a common element in the multinational companies of today.

Multinational companies with operations of various forms and size have mushroomed in virtually every country in the world. American companies have been at the forefront of this expansion. During the period 1950–1976 U.S. direct investment abroad increased more than tenfold. When manufacturing investment alone is considered, the increase is approximately 16-fold.

The international operations of many U.S. companies are now as important and in some cases more important than their domestic operations. "International" nowadays exerts a significant influence on the overall performance of multinational companies. In a recent review of *Fortune* 500 companies, 162 were found to be internationally oriented with more than 25% of sales, earnings, assets, employment, or production outside the United States. A further 129 companies had significant operations outside the United States (between 10–25% of sales, earnings, assets, employment, or production outside the United States).

The environment that a multinational is exposed to is entirely different from the environment in which it works in the United States. In fact, each continent and each country within that continent is a *unique business environment*. A company in a foreign country is exposed to a different political and legal system. Systems vary from a well-defined and elaborate system understandable to the American manager to a complex group of unwritten laws based on *tradition*, or a system whereby a body of people or a single person has the power to make significant changes.

An American company is exposed to the world of *foreign exchange* . . . a world where a dollar has a different value at different times . . . a world where a dollar has different values at the same time.

The international world is a world of different societies and *cultures*. When dealing outside the United States, the human element becomes more important, and even more difficult and complex to tackle. Nevertheless, understanding this human element is essential to every international company in the conduct of its operations in different foreign countries.

Many situations faced by a U.S. company will be the same whether it acquired another U.S. company or an international company. However, in achieving one of the objectives of the acquisition, that is, integrating the management accounting and reporting systems, the acquirer is bound to face situations that are very different from those faced in the United States. Certain important characteristics of a multinational environment have been briefly addressed above.

This section aims to bring forth issues that should be kept in mind when integrating the systems of a newly acquired international company. Since many of the problems are the same as faced with domestic companies, the issues raised here should be addressed along with those discussed in different parts of this book. Furthermore, the issues raised here highlight areas of potential differences. Situations faced will be different depending on the companies involved, the countries involved, and the management styles of the different people involved. Therefore, solutions will be different depending on each particular situation.

PLANNING AND PERIODIC REVIEW OF THE INTEGRATION

The planning of the integration process to a great extent will be influenced by the circumstances leading to the acquisition. A merger that has been thrust upon the acquired company's management will need a different approach than that of a friendly and mutually acceptable takeover. The planning process has to take into consideration the preacquisition activities and atmosphere. Furthermore, the planning of the integration will need to comply with and be heavily influenced by the objectives of the acquisition and the management style of the company—centralized or decentralized as previously discussed.

In the international context one must keep in mind the different cultures of the people involved, in addition, of course, to the different cultures of the companies involved. Accordingly, the overall process becomes more complicated. It is essential that in the planning of the integration process, management of the international company being acquired be involved in as much depth as possible.

The integration of the management accounting and reporting systems must, at the planning stage, be properly and accurately *defined in terms of time frame*. In developing the time frame, an important point to be kept in mind is that too rapid a change might be detrimental to the takeover in the long run. Parent company management must take into consideration the effect change will have on the culture of the acquired company. Time is of less essence in various parts of the world than in the United States. This does not mean that essential items of control need not be introduced; nor does it mean that the parent should not start making changes in the acquired company's system of reporting or control.

With the assistance and participation of the acquired company's management, a suitable timetable can be developed to implement the integration of the acquired company system in order to achieve the objectives of the parent company. Because the integration of the system of the two companies could take a significant amount of time, the whole process must have built-in periodic reviews of progress to date. This is an important step in the cycle for a successful integration. This procedure will enable parent company management to make appropriate changes to the strategy developed in the planning stages. It will also enable acquired company management to give its valuable input to achieve a common and successful objective. The review process should be conducted at regular and constant intervals so that potential problems can be properly addressed at an early stage.

THE HUMAN ELEMENT

The problems and concerns discussed in the previous sections are going to be present whether the acquiree is an American company or an international company. There is bound to be an effect, generally for the worse, on the morale and productivity of the acquired company. Even the most friendly and mutually acceptable takeovers can lead to *uncertainty and personal and emotional stress*. Personnel in the acquired company in all probability will *feel threatened by possible changes*.

This kind of effect is easily evidenced in the international world where the acquiring company may be viewed as an unfriendly foreign multinational. One must accept and be prepared to deal with foreigners reacting differently than Americans in this period of real or perceived change in the acquired company. An acquisition, if it is to be successful, *always entails a substantial amount of change in both* the acquired company and in the parent, although to a lesser degree.

The human element, therefore, becomes an increasingly important factor in determining the success of an acquisition in the international world.

Some of the thoughts expressed below will be applicable whatever the type of acquisition and whether or not the acquiring company is working in a centralized or decentralized environment. Of course, the extent to which the financial accounting and management reporting systems need to be changed will have an effect on the people of the acquired company.

A primary objective of the integration process should be *maintaining the confidence and trust* of the people in the acquired company. In effect, to be successful this is a two-way process. Since foreigners could and most probably will react in different ways, the acquiring company financial management must be extremely sensitive to the needs and fears of all levels of the acquired company's financial management. Among the factors influencing the mutual confidence between acquirer and acquiree is the ability of the parent company managers to develop a personal relationship with the managers of the acquired company. This personal relationship includes all activities other than the actual business on hand. In different countries this period is the sizing-up period where people are weighing each other; a positive association at this stage could have a very favorable impact on the business over the long run. For example, among the Arab and South American countries such as in Brazil, much time is spent developing a strong relationship of trust before business can begin. This is true to a great extent in many other countries in the world and should be emphasized to American financial managers.

In order to develop confidence and trust between the managements of the parent and the newly acquired subsidiary, the responsibility of integration of the financial aspects should be given to a responsible financial manager, preferably of the acquired company. Of course, this should be done in conjunction with corporate financial management. Assigning responsibility to the acquired company management, as it relates to the new company, will to a great extent increase the smoothness with which changes are accepted by local financial management. This will also enable delineation of duties. The financial manager from the parent company should be part of the group with responsibility for the integration of the new controls or system. An advisory capacity for the parent company manager with local responsibility to the acquired company manager seems a preferable approach to giving complete authority to the parent company manager.

The financial management of the acquired company may be apprehensive of the controls and procedures being introduced by the parent company. Acquired company management must be made comfortable with the changes that are planned. This involves the proper education of acquired company management with the *philosophy of the parent company*. On a broad level this relates to whether the company is a centralized or decentralized company, to what extent local company financial management has the authority to carry out its responsibilities, and the method by which the parent company controls its subsidiaries. The important point here is the transfer of knowledge of the parent company to acquired company financial management. This requires a proper training framework for local company management. A proper approach to training could be the difference between imposed parent company controls and mutually accepted parent company controls. In the international context a *visit by acquired company management to corporate headquarters* and meetings with relevant corporate financial management immediately after the acquisition will undoubtedly go a long way toward a smooth transition.

SOCIAL, POLITICAL, AND ECONOMIC EFFECTS

As mentioned previously, a company involved in international business is operating in a multitude of environments, each unique in its own way. The multinational company learns to work within the framework of these environments, while at the same time keeping within the culture and credo of the company, and operating within the laws and regulations by which it is bound, namely both the American and local laws.

A takeover of a company in a foreign country by an American company is bound to affect local social and political circles. In order to minimize the negative effects, corporate management must ensure that its newly acquired subsidiary *keeps within the limits of all local laws and practices* and obtains any approvals that might be necessary. This could be rather difficult at times since it could involve the disclosure of certain parent company information that might not otherwise be publicly available. The parent company will also need to deal with local antitrust bodies. This might be the case when the newly acquired company is in the same country as another operating subsidiary of the parent company. Some countries like to see consolidated information of all companies owned by the same parent, while in other countries the concept of consolidation does not exist or is not allowed.

Special situations must be recognized. For example, companies must be aware of the European Economic Community (EEC) and the directives that it has issued. These directives are addressed to member states and are binding through the national laws of the country when formulated. Certain aspects of the EEC's company law harmonization program will have major implications for companies. The objective of this program is to harmonize "company laws" and establish uniformity in accounting. The two most important directives are the Fourth Directive—Principles of Accounting and Disclosure—and the Seventh Directive—Consolidated Financial Statements (1983).

The Fourth Directive provides a framework of common standards of accounting disclosure for companies subject to the jurisdiction of member countries. The Fourth Directive is still to be implemented in a number of countries. The Seventh Directive, issued in June 1983, has created a framework of rules relating to the consolidation of financial statements for groups of companies. Member countries are expected to introduce legislation to comply with this directive by January 1, 1988.

Companies should also be aware of Articles 85 and 86 of the Treaty of Rome which deal with the EEC competition laws. Their purpose is to ensure that the common market functions as a unified free enterprise economy. Penalties are quite severe for any violations. The parent company having more than one subsidiary in the EEC must ensure compliance by the newly acquired subsidiary of the EEC competition laws. These regulations are quite complicated and need expert legal advice for proper implementation. For example, a company cannot prevent its customer from reselling its products to a market covered by a sister operating company.

U.S. companies must also be aware of both U.S. antitrust laws and similar laws in other countries. Generally, antitrust laws in other countries are different and more liberal than in the United States. There have been cases where a U.S. company's acquisition of a foreign company was blocked by U.S. antitrust laws as well as by the Federal Trade Commission.

The parent company must ensure that payments in the nature of bribes, which are in contravention of U.S. laws, are not being made by its newly acquired subsidiaries. Each company will have its own procedures to implement this, but the parent company needs local company management cooperation in achieving its objectives. In addition to the work done by internal and external auditors, local company management must be asked to make statements that its subsidiaries have complied with the Foreign Corrupt Practices Act in relation to payments made to third parties.

International Boycott Reporting

During the middle to late seventies, a number of laws relating to international boycott activity were introduced in the United States. These laws were introduced as part of the Tax Reform Act as well as the Export Administration Act. Under the tax act there are several provisions that result in a loss of tax benefits for U.S. companies who participate directly or indirectly through their U.S. or international affiliates in an international boycott. The U.S. Treasury provides a list of boycotting countries; however, any country could be deemed to be a boycotting country if it requires boycotting activity.

The boycott laws should be taken seriously as they could have disastrous effects on a corporation since the action taken by one subsidiary could jeopardize the business of the entire corporation. When integrating the reporting systems of acquired companies, parent company management must ensure that the company is not doing anything, even inadvertently, that might detrimentally affect worldwide business.

The activities that are considered boycott activities differ under the two acts. The details and implications of various boycott activities are too complex to discuss here. However, information on worldwide activities relating to gross sales receipts, purchases, and payroll costs will need to be obtained to comply with the tax laws. Similar information will be required to comply with the boycott activities aspects of the Export Administration Act. Further, the operating company will need to make the parent aware of any sales that are deemed to be related to a boycotting company. Parent company objective must be to ensure that the newly acquired subsidiary is familiar and properly understands the effect and implications of any boycott-related activity.

FINANCIAL ISSUES

Financial Statements

The review of the financial statements of an international company is even more important than that of a domestic company. This review is a combination of items that are included in the acquired company's financial statements and items that are excluded from the financials.

Certain differences would have been highlighted during the acquisition process by auditors and specialists familiar with the country's accounting and financial policies and procedures. However, one must keep in mind that the objectives of a preacquisition review are very different from those of a review conducted at the integration stage.

Even though a number of problems are similar whether the acquirer is an American company or a foreign company, the emphasis placed on tackling various issues will probably be different, taking into account the differences of doing business in an international environment. Furthermore, the tools available in resolving potential or perceived problems, as well as the methods used, can be expected to be different.

Certain parts of this section may be the same as mentioned in other sections in this book. The objective of discussing them in this section, at the cost of possible repetition, is to emphasize the areas requiring special attention when the acquisition is international in nature.

The acquisition of a company can lead eventually to changing the company's financials to reflect policies followed by the parent, especially when the parent consolidates the newly acquired company. This will lead to a number of adjustments to the subsidiary financial statements for internal management reporting purposes. In a number of cases this will lead to developing a set of financial statements for management purposes that are different from the financial statements used for local statutory purposes. In certain instances this could mean that an acquired company needs to have a third set of financials. This could happen if the financial statements for tax purposes in the local country already differ from the financial statements used for statutory reporting.

It has been said that in the United States the income statement is of paramount importance, with little attention being paid to the balance sheet of a company. Students of accounting exposed to accounting disciplines in the United States and in some other countries will probably agree. In most of Europe, Asia, and Latin America the balance sheet is considered the most important statement, reflecting major concern in these countries over ownership of wealth (as distinct from the generation of income).

This part of the chapter highlights some important accounting policies that differ from generally accepted accounting policies followed by the parent. Even though reporting for management and internal purposes may be changed to reflect parent company generally accepted accounting principles (GAAP), management must be aware that differences exist in local company reporting and they vary from country to country.

Statutory Audit Requirements

Many countries have statutory audit requirements whereby the financial statements of a company must be audited by local auditors and officially filed with local authorities. These financial statements are generally prepared under local accounting policies and procedures rather than GAAP, under which financial statements for overall corporate purposes are prepared. For example, in the United Kingdom the directors of a company must file a copy of the accounts with the Registrar of Companies within a certain period of time, whether or not the company is a public or private company. In many countries statutory audited financials for 100% owned subsidiaries are required if the company needs local central bank approval to remit dividends to its parent or to remit interest on intercompany borrowings. These requirements differ from the requirements of local company creditors who might insist on company financials based on local accounting policies. In most instances global banks will accept internal management financials based on GAAP. This can save substantial amounts of audit fees if statutory financials are not required for any purpose.

Local Country Foreign Exchange Laws

Depending on the country of acquisition, the parent company may have already faced situations of dealing with local country foreign exchange laws. Unlike in a domestic acquisition, the company is faced with making adjustments to its normal operating procedures due to the presence of country exchange laws.

These laws will impact the way a company finances its new business. A company might have to change its policies where local laws do not allow intercompany borrowings and the company policy is to borrow worldwide from the cheapest source and to fund its worldwide subsidiaries. It will affect the company's normal dividend policies since each country has different regulations related to the remittance of dividends. For example, in a number of Latin American countries that are members of the Andean Common Market, repatriation of profit is limited to a percentage of direct foreign investment and all remittances need central bank approval in advance. In other countries governments might insist on the company meeting certain export commitments. Overall, U.S. companies could be faced with more restrictive regulations which will impact their global strategies.

The local country foreign exchange laws will also affect the parent company approach to charging royalties or technical service fees or for a reimbursement of costs incurred at the head office. All such payments require local central bank approval and if questioned will require adequate substantiation and backup prior to remittance. Payments of this nature are being questioned by more and more countries, specifically in the developing world. Many countries have already introduced legislation eliminating any remittances of such a nature.

Currencies

The acquisition of an international company as compared to a domestic company adds a new dimension to the accounting and management reporting of the parent company. The acquiree is operating in a different environment with its financial records in a currency which is different from its parent. This would create no problems if the value of the foreign currency in dollar terms stayed the same over long periods of time. Since this is highly unlikely in the current international environment, different currencies and the management of subsidiaries with different currencies is part of the problem that multinational companies face on a day-to-day basis.

The uncertain environment surrounding currencies has been particularly prevalent during the last few years. Devaluation of currencies of over 100% was very difficult to believe if not to accept only a few years ago. Zaire devalued its currency in 1983 by about 500% (to approximately 20% of its former value). The currencies of Brazil, Argentina, and a number of other Latin American countries have been steadily decreasing in value. The value of the Portuguese escudo has steadily declined on a monthly basis; additionally, major one-time devaluations have been instituted. During the past few years the dollar has been gaining in strength against a number of international currencies such as the pound sterling, mark, and franc.

Since the parent company financials are in dollars, the financial statements of the acquired company, which are also prepared under GAAP, must be converted into dollars. Therefore, a change in the exchange rate between the company's currency and the dollar will have an impact on the dollar-denominated financial statements of the acquiree. Depending on the change in the rates and the determination of functional currency as covered by Financial Accounting Standards (FAS) 52, the income statement as well as the equity section of the balance sheet of the parent could be significantly impacted. The details of the translation process and the GAAP effect of translations are covered in a later section. The objective of discussing this topic here is to emphasize the potential difference between a domestic and an international acquisition.

A number of countries have more than one exchange rate, and at times it is difficult to decide as to the appropriate rate for accounting purposes. Mexico had two sets of exchange rates—one fixed by the central bank and the other a floating-market rate. Since different rates are used for different purposes, it becomes quite difficult at times to interpret government policies as to the appropriate rate for a particular transaction. South Africa had two exchange rates for some time—a financial rand and a commercial rand. Egypt has three exchange rates—one an official rate for government translation purposes only, a second for official commercial and financial transactions, and a third which is the official open-market rate set regularly by market demand and supply factors.

Based on developments in the recent past, many currencies have been declining rapidly in value in relation to the dollar. This is evidenced in South America where there has been a constant one-way decline as opposed to upward and downward movement against the dollar. Management must recognize this phenomenon and work toward developing strategies to minimize the potential effects of declining currencies.

Financial management must also determine to what extent they would seek protection against foreign exchange risk. The action will depend on the management policies of the parent company; basically, which company should bear the risk will depend on how the company is structured, a centralized or decentralized corporation. If the acquired company and other subsidiaries are being evaluated only in terms of local currency and if most of the operating cash flows are in local currency, there is no incentive on local company management to eliminate any kind of exchange risk.

Management will need to decide what kind of risks to cover and whether the costs of covering the risk justify the benefits. Various methods and instruments available include hedging, leading and lagging of funds transfer, bank-to-bank loans, currency swaps, as well as instruments specific to a particular country, for example, dollar-denominated bonds.

Ethical Considerations

An important aspect of financial statements of American companies is that they must conform to GAAP. The accounting policies in many countries, for various reasons, have not developed, nor are as definitive, as the accounting policies in the United States. This raises the possibility of ethical considerations as they relate to the income statement. Certain foreign companies can adjust earnings by making adjustments to "reserves," which are permissible by local accounting policies. Based on the limited disclosure required, it is not possible to identify these situations on reviewing a company's financial statements. It is also possible under this method to adjust earnings so as to avoid wide fluctuations between years. Therefore, at the time of integration of the financial statements of the acquiree with the parent, this issue should be carefully studied so as to eliminate the possibility of adjusting reserve accounts after the integration has been finalized.

Reserves

In the United States the stockholders' equity section of a balance sheet is generally composed of share capital, additional paid in capital, and retained earnings. In foreign countries local policies require the setting up of reserves. Some of these reserves are specific to a particular purpose, but a general reserve category also exists. In the United Kingdom companies can revalue certain assets, and the resulting surplus is credited to a reserve account. There reserves are not distributable as are some reserves in certain other countries, which must be created because retained earnings may not be distributed as profits.

Inventory

Other countries have differing policies as they relate to inventory. When integrating an acquisition, this area is one that requires careful review. Even though preaudit reviews might have identified differences, the implementation of changes at a detailed level could be quite complex. In most countries the basis of valuing inventories is disclosed, and in a majority of cases inventories are carried at cost or market, whichever is lower. In some countries, unlike in the United States, inventories cannot be valued using the LIFO method for any purposes. This may pose a potential problem to a U.S. company acquiring a company abroad if it values its inventories under the LIFO method in the United States. One of the solutions is to value inventories under the LIFO method in the United States and under FIFO for the valuation of inventories in the foreign companies.

Property, Plant, and Equipment Depreciation

Accounting procedures permitted within GAAP make this topic a potentially complex item for domestic acquisitions as well as for international acquisitions. Lives of assets and depreciation policies vary from country to country, as they do keeping within GAAP. Furthermore, local country regulations may restrict the lives of certain assets. Local tax regulations in certain countries, for example, Kenya, do not allow depreciation but require capital allowances for statutory accounting purposes.

Revaluation of fixed assets is another area where differences exist as compared to GAAP. Many countries permit the revaluation of fixed assets on an ongoing basis with a credit to capital reserve accounts for the realized surplus. In most cases the reserves thus created cannot be utilized for declaring cash dividends but can be utilized for the purpose of stock dividends. Another difference relates to the capitalization of interest costs for construction in progress.

The method of accounting for leases is often different among countries. Capitalization of leases and reflecting capitalized leases on the balance sheet is not a very common policy. Related to this is the fact that commitments for future years under lease-and-hire purchase contracts need not be disclosed in many countries.

Depreciation policies also vary between countries, with the straight-line method of depreciation being the most common. Accelerated methods of depreciation are not permitted by many countries and even if they are permitted are not practiced widely. In a number of countries, for example, Greece and Germany, the method of depreciation for book purposes must comply with the method used for tax purposes and permitted by local tax regulations. When fixed assets are revalued, it is also important to determine if the depreciation charged on revaluation is charged directly to the capital reserve account or flows through income.

Taxes

Chapter 8 deals with taxes. Tax laws in every country are bound to be different, and local company management and local tax experts are in the best position to advise the parent company on local tax issues. However, U.S. financial management must also be aware that accounting in international companies may differ from GAAP as it relates to taxes. A provision for deferred tax purposes is not permitted in a number of countries. For example, in Germany and Greece, accounting practices adhere strictly to tax requirements. In certain countries because of differences between local tax regulations and parent company accounting policies a deferred tax account will be created.

Research and Development Costs

This is another important accounting area where differences exist between GAAP and local country accounting regulations. Similar differences existed in the United States until FAS 2 was issued, which stated that all research and development costs were required to be expensed in the year incurred and not capitalized for amortization in future years except under certain specified situations. Certain countries still permit the capitalization of such costs with amortization over future periods.

REPORTING

Periods

An objective of the integration would be to have the acquiree follow the same reporting schedule developed by the parent company for its other subsidiaries. This is a potential problem, the impact of which should not be underestimated.

The reporting problems relate to two major items: reporting of actual results on a regular basis and the reporting of forecasts for management budgeting and consolidation purposes. The newly acquired subsidiary which is operating on a different basis than the parent must adapt to the corporate reporting calendar. Among factors to be taken into consideration is the comparability of prior data, possible restatement of prior-period data, and even the possibility of having separate reporting for local company management and for corporate reporting. Of course, the last item mentioned may cause a lot of confusion and therefore should be avoided wherever possible.

This problem becomes bigger when the acquired subsidiary has different subsidiaries or operating units in various countries. This could be the case when the acquiree is a Germany company with manufacturing locations in a couple of different German cities as well as in other European countries. In this case a change to the corporate reporting schedule will necessitate a change all the way down the line. Such a change will be difficult to accomplish if it is not planned and implemented over a period of time.

Changes are easier when only a limited amount of information is requested. This is the case when the parent wants sales and income amounts only. When it comes to more detailed information, it must be remembered that different countries could follow different accounting terminology, thereby making the transition a more difficult and time-consuming process. The classification of expenses, for example, between distribution and administration is different between companies in the United States. These differences could be much wider when comparing the same classifications between an American and an international company.

A similar problem is faced when integrating the management reporting system for the forecasting cycles. An acquired company may be preparing forecasts on a different time schedule, say, only one year in the future. The well-managed parent may be requesting its subsidiaries for one-year, two-year, and five-year forecasts. Changing the acquiree's system for longer-term reporting for management purposes requires a change in attitudes perhaps stretching far beyond the acquired financial and accounting department's capabilities. This is a slow evolutionary process, one of change, and requires a well-thought-out plan to be implemented successfully.

Systems and Communications

During the past 10 years the United States has seen an explosion in the information processing field. The advent of personal computers, word processors, facsimile machines, and other office automation tools has impacted the financial and management reporting systems of most American companies. A parallel development has also been witnessed to a great extent in the rest of the developed world, especially in Europe. A few other countries in the world—Brazil, Australia, Hong Kong—have also been engulfed in this rapid change, but to different extents.

The problem of incompatibility of computer systems that an American parent faces with its newly acquired international subsidiary will probably be similar to that faced in acquiring a domestic company. Of course, this assumes that the parent company and its subsidiaries have an interconnected computer system through which information can be readily exchanged. The problems in the international world are more than likely related to the possibility of nonexistence of computers in the subsidiary or of computers and a system that does not have the sophistication of the American parent company's system. This could lead to potential delays if the parent has tight reporting deadlines. Companies in many countries might still be on a manual system or on a partially automated system. These systems will need to be improved, even if not fully computerized. Such a change will definitely take time, keeping in mind that one of the objectives is that the integrity of the data should not be affected.

Communication of management and financial information to the parent company for internal or consolidation purposes is a problem likely to be faced on the international front. The United States has an excellent telephone system, which makes for a good backup system if information cannot be transmitted through interconnected computers. Many companies have a worldwide computer and information network. The telephone system is the primary means of using this communication system. Since the telephone systems of many developing countries have a long way to go toward reaching American standards, proper attention must be given to this problem when utilizing an interconnected worldwide information gathering network. The telex system is used widely by companies to gather financial information from international subsidiaries. This has its usual pitfalls when the telex line is not operating, along with the telephone system, and the subsidiary cannot contact the parent to send in its regular report. In such instances backup plans must be in place so that one subsidiary does not hold up consolidated reports. Using a forecast instead of actual numbers is one of the approaches to overcoming this problem if the subsidiary does not have a major effect on the consolidated total.

Communications, on the whole, in the international world are not as well developed as in the United States. However, things are changing very rapidly, and in a few years we can expect new means of communication in different parts of the developing world. Improvements have taken place in a number of spheres. The development of worldwide courier systems and the development of quick facsimile machines, differing computers communicating with each other, and satellite transmissions are only a few of the improvements that are affecting the international communication of information. Meanwhile, some countries still have restrictions on transmission of financial data which may affect the ability to communicate financial data.

INTERNATIONAL IN THE FUTURE

The complexities of dealing with international companies will probably increase in the future. The changes in the world political and economic system will have their impact on each country. Additionally, the development of political and economic systems internally within individual countries will have a tremendous impact in that country.

Locally imposed regulations on international companies are expected to increase and complicate the global activity of multinational countries. This is especially so in the developing world with economic orders and systems different from those found in the United States and Europe. Fluctuating exchange rates, central bank, and local political intervention and control will continue to be part of doing business internationally. Multinational developments, at the same time, should bring more harmony and commonality to international accounting developments. The European Economic Community through its directives, is moving toward achieving this goal. The International Federation of Accountants and the International Accounting Standards Committee are working toward developing a worldwide accounting profession and international accounting standards. Combined with the above are the developments in communications that are essential to the management of multinational companies. The future in the international scene is therefore expected to become more challenging.

CONCLUSION

The international environment is different from the environment in the United States. Countries in various parts of the world are unique in their own ways, and parent company financial management must take this into consideration when developing a comprehensive plan for the integration of newly acquired international companies. These plans, which must be reviewed on a periodic basis, need to be flexible to reflect different circumstances in countries but still achieve the objectives of the parent company in the overall integration process.

The human element is considered even more important in the international context. Working with local financial management, where thinking and philosophies may be different, is essential. In order to achieve this, a good training and education program is quite essential. The transition with international companies should also reflect the differences in cultures, especially as it relates to time. A well-developed slow change can achieve the objectives of an acquisition much better than a hastily and quickly implemented integration.

CHECKLIST

The checklist below is not comprehensive in itself. These items should be included in conjunction with the checklists that appear elsewhere in this book.

1. *Developing Integration Plan*
   (a) Responsibility: Corporate and local company
   (b) Integration plan schedule
   (c) Periodic progress reviews
   (d) Local company employee training and education
2. *Financial Statements*
   (a) Statutory
   (b) Local tax purposes
   (c) Parent company GAAP
3. *Accounting Issues*
   (a) Reserves
   (b) Inventory
   (c) Property, Plant and Equipment, and Depreciation
   (d) Taxes
   (e) Research and development costs
   (f) Foreign currency and related issues
4. *External*
   (a) Local regulations
   (b) Antitrust/monopoly bodies
   (c) International issues (EEC Directives etc.)
   (d) Foreign exchange laws
5. *U.S. Legal Requirements*
   (a) FCPA
   (b) Arab boycott
   (c) Antitrust

(d) FTC

(e) Other

6. *Internal*

(a) Reporting periods: Actual and forecast

(b) Reporting via

(1) Telex

(2) Telephone

(3) Facsimile

(4) Direct interface with computer system

(5) Other

seven

CONSOLIDATION AND EXTERNAL REPORTING

Joseph L. Fischer, CPA

CONTENTS

INTRODUCTION

The process of integrating acquisitions can impose a significant reporting burden for the acquired company when external reporting requirements must be adhered to, particularly if the acquired company was a nonpublic company prior to the acquisition. It is imperative to consider how best to accumulate this information with a minimum of effort on the part of the acquired company while still ensuring the integrity of the information. Particular attention must be given to the size of the acquired company, the sophistication of its reporting systems, and the quality and experience of its staff. Every effort must be made to use the existing reporting systems and information to satisfy the reporting requirements.

Since the external reporting requirements are enormous and vary from industry to industry, this chapter describes a process that can be followed by most companies which takes the local currency financial statements, converts the information to a consolidation format, and describes the alternatives in the consolidation process, which subsequently results in the published consolidated financial statements of the reporting entity. The final section will address the key disclosure requirements that are pertinent to the acquisition.

It is important to note that due to the vast reporting requirements of U.S. generally accepted accounting principles (GAAP) and the extensive reporting requirements of the Securities and Exchange Commission, the reader must consult the official promulgated rules before completing the planning process of integrating an acquisition. This chapter will assist management accountants in developing the integration plan and identifying some of the critical areas that may be overlooked.

FOREIGN CURRENCY TRANSLATION

The acquisition of an international company poses certain difficulties from an internal reporting aspect, especially the conversion of the local currency financial statements into the reporting currency, for our purposes U.S. dollars. While many internal management reporting requirements are satisfied by local currency financial statements, it is obvious that local company performance will usually be measured in one currency. The process of translation has been debated for many years and recently FAS 52, "Accounting for the Translation of Foreign Currency Transactions and Foreign Currency Financial Statements," has attempted to resolve the conflict. Some corporations have used different translation methods for internal reporting than for external. SFAS 52 allows a company to determine the method of translation based on the operational aspects of the business and to use the basic underlying economic issues to determine the best method.

Before attempting to translate the local financial statements to U.S. dollars, the functional currency of the acquired company must be selected. The functional currency may be the local currency, the currency of the reporting entity, or some other currency. The functional currency that would be used for the acquired company can be changed as a result of the acquisition due to a change in financing, intercompany transactions, and a general change in cash flows. Specifically, the FASB has stated that the functional currency is a matter of fact and defines an entity's functional currency as the currency of the primary economic environment in which the entity operates; normally, that is the currency in which an entity primarily generates and expends cash.

The FASB has identified specific functional currency indicators that must be reviewed when determining the functional currency. They are:

1. *Cash Flow.* Are cash flows of the acquired company's assets and liabilities primarily in a foreign currency or do they have a direct impact on the cash flows of the parent company.

2. *Sales Price.* Are sales prices of the acquired company responsive to short-term changes in exchange rates determined by global competition or local competition and government regulations.

3. *Sales Market.* Is there an active local sales market or is the sales market in the parent's country.

4. *Expenses.* Are cost of goods and operating expenses primarily local costs or are they primarily influenced by the parent company or some other currency.

5. *Financing.* In what currency is the company's financing denominated in and does the company have sufficient funds to service debt obligations.

6. *Intercompany Transactions.* How extensive is the interrelationship between the parent and the subsidiary and its other affiliates.

The indicators obviously make good business sense in terms of identifying which currency affects your business the most. After determination of the functional currency, the local statements are remeasured on this basis.

Once the local statements are expressed in the functional currency, it is then time to translate them to the reporting currency to accommodate the consolidation. The translation process is simply a method of converting to a common unit, and gains and losses that arise as a result of the change in the relationship of the common unit are deferred to the balance sheet. The local functional currency financial statements are translated at the current exchange rate. Revenues, expenses, gains and losses are translated at the exchange rates at the dates when the transactions are recognized; a weighted-average rate for the period may be used.

The assets and liabilities are translated at the current end of period rate, with any gain or loss that arises as a result of changes in the exchange rate charged to a separate account in the equity section. Capital accounts are translated at the historical rates. This facilitates the elimination of the investment account in the consolidation process.

Translation of results in highly inflationary economies requires that the financial statements be measured as if the functional currency were the reporting currency. This method basically follows FAS 8, with the resulting exchange gains and losses included in income. A highly inflationary economy is one having cumulative inflation of approximately 100% or more over a three-year period.

Any goodwill that arises from an acquisition or other revaluation of assets and liabilities will also be translated under the current rate method.

After the accounts have been translated to the reporting currency, the consolidation process can begin. The translation process can be performed at the local level or at the parent company. The selection of a method really depends on the makeup of both organizations. Regardless of the method used, it is important to maintain local currency financial statements and precise analyses of the effects currency exchange rates have on the U.S. dollar statements.

CONSOLIDATION PROCESS

The purpose of consolidated statements is to present the combined results of a total entity as if it were one company. This immediately raises questions regarding the types of businesses, the percent of ownerships, the interrelated transactions of the group, the effects of foreign companies, and the valuation of the assets at the time of the acquisition. The generally accepted accounting principles for business combinations are covered by APB 16, "Accounting of Business Combinations," and FAS 38, "Accounting for Preacquisition Contingencies of Purchased Enterprises."

There are two acceptable methods of accounting for business combinations; one is the "purchase" method the other is the "pooling of interests" method. The methods are not choices but are determined based on criteria outlined in APB 16.

The purchase method is similar to the purchase of an asset. The company expends funds and acquires an asset that it will use in its business. The pooling method is in essence two entities combining and using their combined resources in the formation of a new company. Practically speaking, a pooling of interest is accomplished with the exchange of shares when a purchase involves primarily cash or funds other than stock.

The specific guidelines for determining the method used as outlined in APB 16 are as follows:

The pooling of interests method requires specific conditions to exist before the method can be used. If an acquisition does not meet these conditions the acquisition is treated as a purchase.

1. Each of the combining companies must be autonomous and not have been a subsidiary or division of another corporation within two years before the plan of combination is initiated.

2. At the date of initiation and at the date of consummation of the plan of combination, each combining company is independent of each other combining company.

3. After a plan is initiated, it must be completed within one year in accordance with a specific plan or completed in a single transaction.

4. At the consummation date of the plan the acquiring company offers and issues its majority class of stock (voting rights) for no less than 90% of the voting common stock interests of the combining company being acquired. The 90% or more of the voting common stock interests being acquired is determined at the date the plan is consummated.

5. None of the combining companies change the equity interest of the voting common stock in contemplation of the combination either within two years before the plan of combination is initiated or between the dates the combination is initiated and consummated; this includes distributions to stockholders and additional issuances, exchanges, and retirements of securities.

6. Shares of voting common stock can only be reacquired for purposes other than business combinations, and no company reacquires more than a normal number of shares between the dates the plan of combination is initiated and consummated.

7. The ratio of the interest of an individual common stockholder to those of other common stockholders in a combining company remains the same as a result of the exchange of stock to effect the combination.

8. The stockholders are neither deprived of nor restricted in exercising the voting rights to which they are entitled.
9. The combination is resolved at the date the plan is consummated.

If all of the conditions of the pooling of interests method are met, the consolidation process is as follows:

1. All of the accounts, assets, liabilities, and stockholders equity are combined at the historical reported costs of the separate entities.
2. The period reported under the consolidation assumes that the combination of entities occurred at the beginning of the period.

There is no goodwill recorded in the consolidation under a pooling of interests.

PURCHASE METHOD

If a business combination is deemed to be a purchase, the business combination is recorded at the acquired cost or fair market value. Any excess of the total purchase price over the fair value of the net assets acquired is recorded as goodwill.

The total cost of an acquisition accounted for under a purchase method is allocated to the individual assets acquired. In many cases appraisal values are needed for property, plant, and equipment; other accounts could be valued as follows:

Inventory.   Net realizable value less a normal profit

Receivables.   Present value or net realizable value

Marketable Securities.   Net realizable value

Liabilities.   Present value

Contingent Assets and Liabilities, FAS 38

FAS 38 requires that any preacquisition contingency defined as a contingency of an enterprise that is acquired in a business combination accounted for by the purchase method be included in the assets or liabilities of the combining company when allocating the purchase price.

Effects of Consolidation

The Exhibits 7.1 and 7.2 indicate the effect of consolidation after the recording of the acquisition.

Exhibit 7.1 Purchase Method Consolidating Workpapers

	Parent Company	Acquired Company	Consolidating Entries Dr.	Consolidating Entries Cr.	Consolidated
Current assets					
Cash	6,000	2,000			8,000
Marketable securities	21,000	6,000			27,000
Accounts receivable	12,000	4,000		500[b]	15,500
Inventories	35,000	11,000			46,000
Prepaid expenses	4,000	1,000			5,000
Property, plant & equip. (net)	92,000	22,000	2,000[a]		116,000
Investments in affiliates	31,000			31,000[a]	0
Goodwill			1,000[a]		1,000
Total Assets	201,000	46,000	3,000	31,500	218,500
Current liabilities					
Accounts payable	18,000	4,000	500[b]		21,500
Income taxes	17,000	7,000			24,000
Long-term debt	88,000	7,000			95,000
Total Liabilities	123,000	18,000	500		140,500
Stockholders' equity					
Common stock	11,000	3,000	3,000[a]		11,000
Capital in excess of par	27,000	15,000	15,000[a]		27,000
Retained earnings	40,000	10,000	10,000[a]		40,000
Total equity	78,000	28,000	28,000		78,000
Total Liabilities & Equity	201,000	46,000	28,500		218,500

[a] To eliminate investment and revalue acquired company's assets.
[b] Eliminate intercompany accounts.

Exhibit 7.2 Pooling Method Consolidating Workpapers

	Parent Company	Acquired Company	Consolidating Entries Dr.	Consolidating Entries Cr.	Consolidated
Current assets					
Cash	6,000	2,000			8,000
Marketable securities	21,000	6,000			27,000
Accounts receivable	12,000	4,000		500[a]	15,500
Inventories	35,000	11,000			46,000
Prepaid expenses	4,000	1,000			5,000
Property, plant & equip. (net)	92,000	22,000			114,000
Investments in affiliates	28,000			28,000[b]	
Total Assets	198,000	46,000		28,500	215,500
Current liabilities					
Accounts payable	18,000	4,000	500[a]		21,500
Income taxes	17,000	7,000			24,000
Long-term debt	88,000	7,000			95,000
Total Liabilities	123,000	18,000	500		140,500
Stockholders' equity					
Common stock	11,000	3,000	3,000[b]		11,000
Capital in excess of par	14,000	15,000	15,000[b]		14,000
Retained earnings	50,000	10,000	10,000[b]		50,000
Total equity	75,000	28,000	28,000		75,000
Total Liabilities & Equity	198,000	46,000	28,500		215,500

[a] Eliminate intercompany accounts.
[b] Eliminate involvement with affiliate.

DISCLOSURE REQUIREMENTS

The disclosure requirements of any public company are enormous, considering U.S. GAAP requirements and the requirements of the Securities and Exchange Commission (SEC). In recent years the SEC has attempted to integrate the reporting of GAAP and SEC requirements to bring them in line and avoid duplicate requirements or different formats for the same information.

The following pages will deal specifically with the public reporting requirements for two important areas—segments and changing prices.

In addition, a listing of the major disclosure items for the form of combination, commitments and contingencies, pensions and lease commitments is presented. Because the lists are so extensive and does change for certain industries, it is critical to review the official text of the SEC and GAAP rules. This section contains the critical disclosure items that arise in the integration of an acquisition.

SEGMENTS

The incorporation of segment information of the acquiree poses a challenge in the integration of an acquisition. Generally, the information is available in product line form and can easily be adapted to the parent's segment reporting. The parent company has presumably developed broad segments of business that the newly acquired company needs to fold into or the total reporting format needs to be restructured.

FAS 14 provides the GAAP for financial reporting for segments of a business enterprise. This statement provides information to assist financial statement users in analyzing and understanding the entities' underlying composition. This seems to be the one statement that has truly provided useful information both to the preparers of financial statements and the users.

Standards for Reporting Segments

Segment information shall be included in published financial statements for the end of the enterprise's fiscal year.

Segment information will include that relating to:

1. The enterprise's operations in different industries.
2. Foreign operations and export sales.
3. Major customers.

Determination of the Reportable Segment

In determining reportable segments of an enterprise you must (1) identify the individual product lines and services, (2) group those product lines by industry segment, and (3) select those industry segments that are significant. The identifiable industry segments must then be integrated with the segments of the combined entity. This may involve the addition of segments or the separation of previously combined segments. Caution must be exercised when extracting product line information from sales data which may be organized by type of sales force or size. For example, a consumer products division may include pharmaceutical sales because of sales or distribution lines. However, in the newly combined entity pharmaceutical sales may be a significant segment that needs to be reported separately. The determination of segments depends on the information and management's judgment.

An entity's existing profit centers are the best place to start in determining industry segments because both revenues and expenses are generally accumulated in these centers.

Only significant industry segments need to be identified as a reportable segment. To determine significance the following tests apply:

1. Revenues are 10% or more of the combined revenue of all of the combined entity's industry segment.
2. Operating profit or loss is 10% or more of the greater of (a) the combined operating profit of all industry segments that were profitable or (b) the combined operating loss of all industry segments that did incur an operating loss.
3. Identifiable assets are 10% or more of the combined identifiable assets of all industry segments.

If any of these tests apply, the segment should be reported separately. The following information is required on each reportable segment.

1. Revenue: sales to unaffiliated customers and sales or transfers to other industry segments shall be separately disclosed.
2. Operating profit or loss.
3. Identifiable assets.
4. Other related disclosures
   a. Depreciation, depletion, and amortization expense
   b. Capital expenditures
   c. Equity in the net income of unconsolidated subsidiaries
   d. Effect on segment operating profit from a change in accounting principle

Also included with the segment information is the information about foreign operations and export sales. Information should be presented for each significant geographical area. The entity should disclose revenue, operating profit or loss, and identifiable assets. Also, when an entity has export sales to third parties, these amounts should be disclosed.

Information About Major Customers. If 10% or more of the revenue of an enterprise is derived from sales to any single customer, that fact and the amount of revenue from each customer shall be disclosed. For purposes of this statement domestic government agencies in aggregate and foreign governments in the aggregate are treated as single customers.

Restatement of Previously Reported Segment Information. Because the segment information is required on a comparative basis, previously reported information must be restated when (1) there is a change in accounting principle or change due to a business combination and (2) when there has been a change in the way the entity's products and services are grouped into industry segments or a change in the way the entity foreign operation are grouped into geographical areas.

FINANCIAL REPORTING AND CHANGING PRICES

The FASB in 1979 issued FAS 33 "Financial Reporting and Changing Prices," which required public enterprises to issue supplementary information about the effects of inflation on their business and its historical cost financial statements. Prior to this statement public companies were required to provide replacement cost information in Form 10-K to the SEC. Statement 33, however, is a more comprehensive disclosure that uses two distinct methods of inflation accounting. The statement has been issued as an experiment to determine the best method of portraying the effects of inflation. The two methods required are the constant-dollar and current-cost methods. Constant-dollar accounting is a method of restating various elements of financial statements in dollars of the same purchasing power. Current cost is a method of revaluing elements of financial statements to the current cost or lower recoverable amount.

Public enterprises that prepare financial statements in U.S. dollars in accordance with U.S. GAAP and that meet the following test are subject to the disclosure requirements:

Companies that have either inventories and gross property, plant, and equipment exceeding $125 million *or* total assets exceeding $1 billion.

The disclosures are required only for consolidated financial statements. The disclosures do not pertain to an entity in the first year of a business combination accounted for as a pooling of interests if neither of the combining companies met the size test before the combination. However, if one of the combining companies met the size test before combining, then the new entity is required to disclose the information.

Disclosures

Entities are required to present the following items on a constant-dollar basis:

Income from continuing operations.
Purchasing power gain or loss on net monetary items.
Any reductions of constant-dollar amounts to a lower recoverable value.

The following information is required on a current-cost basis:

Income from continuing operations. Current costs of inventory, property, plant, and equipment. Increase or decrease in the current cost of inventory and property, plant, and equipment net of inflation for the current period.

A five-year summary of selected financial data is required and includes:

1. Net sales and other operating revenues.
2. Historical cost/constant-dollar information for:
   (a) Income from continuing operations.
   (b) Income per common share from continuing operations.
   (c) Net assets at year-end.
   (d) Increase or decrease in the current cost of inventories and property, plant, and equipment net of inflation.
3. Other information:
   (a) Purchasing power gain or loss on net monetary items.
   (b) Cash dividends declared per common share.
   (c) Market price per common share at year-end.

FAS 70 amends FAS 33 and specifies that an enterprise that measures a significant part of its operations in functional currencies other than the U.S. dollar is exempted from FAS 33 requirements to present constant-dollar information. Operations that have functional currencies other than the U.S. dollar should measure current-cost amounts and increases or decreases therein in the functional currency.

Exhibit 7.3 Company Name (Indicate Country) Current Cost Data For the Year Ending _____ *(000's local currency)*

Duplicate Cols. 1–5 In All Cards Line Name	Line No.	Historical Cost (A)	Line No.	Current Cost (B)
	6–8	9–19	6–8	9–19
Gross Value				
Land and land improvements	401		501	
Building and building equipment	402		502	
Machinery and equipment	403		503	
Leasehold improvements	404		504	
Construction in progress	405		505	
Total	410		510	
Net Book Value				
Land and land improvements	412		512	
Building and building equipment	413		513	
Machinery and equipment	414		514	
Leasehold improvements	415		515	
Construction in progress	416		516	
Total	420		520	
Depreciation Expense				
Land and land improvements	422		522	
Building and building equipment	423		523	
Machinery and equipment	424		524	
Leasehold improvements	425		525	
Total	430		530	
Inventory (B)				
Raw materials and supplies	432		532	
Work in process	434		534	
Finished goods	436		536	
Total	440		540	
Cost of Sales (C)	450		550	

(A) Indicate the gross and net value of permanent idle capacity included in the historical numbers and excluded in current cost calculations:

GROSS: _____ NET: _____

An acquired company that has not been reporting this information will require significant staff training to develop reliable disclosures. However, the process of reporting can be simplified by use of appropriately designed reporting forms, as shown in Exhibit 7.3 and 7.4.

The additional disclosures can be prepared at the consolidated level without significant input from subsidiaries.

Exhibit 7.4   Company Name (Indicate Country) Current Cost Data For the Year Ending _____ (000's local currency)

Itemized Adjustments (per exhibit 7.3)

		Raw Materials & Supplies	Work in Process	Finished Goods
(B)	*Inventory*			
	Historical cost	$1,000	$1,000	$2,000
	Adjustments (itemize);			
	Restate LIFO to FIFO	(LIFO companies only)		
	Excess, obsolete & discontinued	(LIFO companies only)		
	Excess of market price over			
	contact price (less than 2 years)	10	10	10
	Current replacement cost	$1,010	$1,010	$2,020

		Total
(C)	*Cost of sales*	
	Historical cost	$7,500
	Adjustments (itemize):	
	Jan. revaluation gain	200
	Excess of market price over	
	contract price (less than 2 years)	80
	LIFO layer absorbed	(LIFO companies only)
	Current replacement cost	$7,780

Index Information

Building & building equipment and leasehold improvements
  Based on Boeckh Modifier (base year 1967) American Appraisal Co., Milwaukee, Wisconsin, issued bimonthly
  September 30, index adjustment by 2.6% estimate to year-end
Machinery & equipment
  Based on Wholesale Price Index (base year 1967) U.S. Bureau of Labor Statistics issued monthly
  October 30, index adjusted by 2.5% estimate to year-end
Land and land improvements
  Services of ABC Realty Appraisal Inc.

DISCLOSURE LIST

The following listing provides the disclosures required that are particularly important in integrating an acquisition. This is not a comprehensive list of disclosures for complete financial statements. It does, however, provide the basis for developing the planning process for collecting information when acquiring and integrating a new company.

Business Combinations

Pooling	Purchase
1. Name and description of the companies combined.	1. Name and description of the acquired company.
2. Method of accounting for the combination.	2. Method of accounting for the combination.
3. Description and number of shares of stock issued in the combination.	3. Cost of the acquired company and value and number of any shares of stock issued.
4. Time period for which income of the acquired company is included in the consolidated statements of the combined entities.	4. Time period for which results of operations of the acquired company are included in the income statement of the acquiring corporation.
5. Any adjustments of net assets of the combining companies to adopt consistent accounting principles.	5. If goodwill is recorded, indicated the method of amortization.
6. If fiscal year of acquired company is changed, indicate the changes in revenues, expenses, extraordinary items, net income, and other changes to stockholder equity.	6. Contingent payments, options or commitments and their accounting treatment.
7. Reconcile the amounts of revenue and earnings previously reported by the acquiring company that issues the stock to effect the combination with the combined amounts currently presented in financial statements and summaries.	7. Pro forma information: (a) Combined income for the current period. (b) Combined income for the immediately preceding period if comparative financial statements are presented.

Commitments and Contingencies

1. Contract commitments and guarantees.
2. Loss contingencies.
3. Direct and indirect guarantees of indebtedness.
4. Unused letters of credit.
5. Accounts receivables with recourse.
6. Litigation cases.
7. Tax contingencies.

Pensions

1. Description of the plan, describing the employees covered.
2. Statement of the company's accounting and funding policies.
3. Pension expense for the periods presented by the financial statements.
4. Matters affecting comparability.
5. For complete sets of financial statements FAS 35 requires:
   (a) Actuarial present value of vested accumulated plan benefits.
   (b) Actuarial present value of nonvested accumulated plan benefits.
   (c) Net assets available for benefits.
   (d) Assumed rate of return used in determining the actuarial present value of vested and nonvested benefits.
   (e) Date used to determine benefit information.

For those plans for which this information is not available, particularly foreign plans, disclose the excess of the actuarially computed value of vested benefits over the total of the pension fund and any balance sheet accruals less any pension prepayments or deferrals. Value of the pension is based on the latest valuation data available.

LEASE COMMITMENTS

Capital Leases

1. Gross amount of assets recorded under capital leases as of date of each balance sheet presented by major classes according to nature or function.

2. Aggregate future minimum lease payments for the balance sheet dates presented and for each of the five succeeding years less executory costs included in minimum lease payments.
3. Imputed interest necessary to reduce the net minimum lease payments to present value.
4. Minimum sublease rentals from noncancelable subleases.
5. Total contingent rentals actually incurred for each period for which an income statement is presented.

Operating Leases

1. Aggregate future minimum rental payments for the periods presented and each of the five succeeding fiscal years.
2. Total minimum rentals to be received in the future under noncancelable subleases.
3. Rental expense for each period presented.

A general description of the leasee's leasing arrangements including basis of contingent rental payments, renewal or purchase options and escalation clauses, restrictions on dividends, additional debt, and further leasing.

Disclosures by Lessors

Sales Type and Direct Financing Leases

1. Components of the net investments in leases:
    (a) Future minimum lease payments less executory costs and allowances for uncollectable minimum lease payments.
    (b) Unguaranteed residual values accruing to the benefit of the lessor.
    (c) Unearned income.
2. Future minimum lease payments for each of the five succeeding periods.
3. Total contingent rentals included in income for each period for which an income statement is presented.
4. Unearned income to offset initial direct costs.

Operating Leases.   General description of the lessor's leasing arrangements.

1. The cost and carrying amount of property on lease by major classes of property according to nature or function, and the amount of accumulated depreciation in total.
2. Aggregate minimum future rentals on noncancelable lease and for each of the five succeeding periods.
3. Total contingent rentals included in income for each period for which an income statement is presented

CHECKLIST

1. Minimize the effort of integrating an acquisition.
2. Selecting functional currency.
3. Translate financial statements.
4. Treatment of goodwill.
5. Consolidation worksheet.
6. Purchase versus pooling method.
7. Effects of consolidation:
   (a) Segments: Disclosure requirements and determining a reportable segment.
   (b) Changing prices: Disclosure requirements and forms.
   (c) Disclosure Items: Pooling versus purchase, commitments and contingencies, pensions, and leases.

eight

TAX ISSUES TO BE RECOGNIZED

Stanley Stern, MBA, CPA

CONTENTS

INITIAL TAX PLANNING

There are many forms the acquisition of one business enterprise by another can take. However, for purposes of financial accounting all acquisitions are classified as either a purchase transaction or a pooling of interests. Requirements for each method are set forth in Accounting Principles Board Opinion 16, "Business Combinations." For federal income tax purposes, the transaction is either taxable or tax-free. Tax-free reorganizations are described in the Internal Revenue Code at Section 368.

The following discussion will briefly compare a tax-free with a taxable acquisition, distinguish a pooling of interests from a tax-free reorganization, and describe the different and often conflicting objectives of the buyer and seller.

Taxable Acquisition versus Tax-Free Reorganization

A transaction will be taxable unless it meets the specific requirements for one of the tax-free reorganizations described in Section 368. A taxable acquisition can take several forms, for example, the buyer can acquire some or all of the assets of the selling enterprise, or some or all of the outstanding capital stock of the enterprise from the current shareholders.

Taxable Acquisition of Stock. If the purchaser buys the stock of the seller, the seller will realize a long-term capital gain or loss, assuming the requisite holding period requirements are met. A long-term capital gain is desirable from the seller's point of view because the highest tax rates currently applicable to capital gains, that is, 20% for an individual shareholder and 28% for a corporate shareholder, compare favorably with the highest tax rates applicable to other forms of income, which are 50 and 46%, respectively. Conversely if the transaction results in a capital loss, the seller may not realize any tax benefit due to limitations in the amount of capital loss that can be used to offset ordinary income. In such case a sale of assets should be considered.

The acquired company's balance sheet reflects the same asset values as were shown before the acquisition. The buyer records the purchase price as an investment. In consolidation for financial reporting purposes, the excess of this investment over the fair market value of the net assets of the acquired company is recorded as goodwill. Goodwill negatively impacts subsequent reported earnings because it must be amortized pursuant to APB Opinion 17. However, goodwill cannot be depreciated or amortized for tax purposes.

The buyer has the option to liquidate or merge the acquired company and assign the excess purchase price to an asset or group of assets that qualify for tax deductions, but the revaluation of assets must be supported on IRS examination. In order to substantiate the allocation of the excess purchase price to undervalued assets, a competent appraisal should be obtained. Rules relating to revaluation of assets are discussed later in this chapter.

Taxable Acquisition of Assets.   If the purchaser buys the assets of the seller, the tax consequences to the seller are more complex than if the seller had sold stock. The selling corporation generally will transfer the assets to the acquiring corporation, liquidate and distribute the sale proceeds to its shareholders.

The shareholders' proceeds received as a result of the complete liquidation of the selling corporation results in capital gain to the extent they exceed the shareholders' tax basis in the stock of the entity sold.

Assuming the corporation adopts a plan of liquidation, and subject to certain exceptions, gain or loss will not be recognized to the selling corporation on the sale of its assets. These exceptions can be quite significant. For example, depreciation previously taken on fixed assets may be recaptured as ordinary income if such assets are sold at a gain. Investment tax credit may also be recaptured if the requisite holding period has not been satisfied by the selling corporation. Recent changes in the tax law also requires recapture of LIFO reserves in certain tax-free liquidations.

The buyer would allocate the purchase price pursuant to the provisions of the contract.

Buyer–Seller Negotiation of Adverse Tax Interests

In addition to resolving possible conflicts between the buyer and seller concerning a taxable or tax-free reorganization, the buyer and seller must negotiate the allocation of the purchase price to the various assets acquired in a taxable acquisition of assets.

One simple example of the disparity of interest that exists between buyer and seller regarding the allocation of proceeds would be the amount allocated to depreciable personal property (e.g., furniture and fixtures, machinery, and equipment) used in the trade or business. The buyer wants most of the proceeds allocated to this category in order to maximize future depreciation deductions for tax purposes, and thereby increase cash flow by decreasing future federal and state tax liabilities. The seller, however, will ordinarily have taxable gain as a result of such an allocation, and even worse, much of that gain can be "recaptured" as ordinary income. The seller would prefer to allocate proceeds to assets which would result in capital gains, rather than to assets that would result in ordinary income.

The buyer would also want to assign current replacement value to assets that could be liquidated most rapidly to recover the invested cash quickly. Therefore, the buyer may desire to assign a high value to inventories as this would provide the most rapid cash recovery. However, excess of proceeds allocated to inventory over seller's cost would generally result in ordinary income, and the seller would be taxed at the ordinary rate on such an allocation. The seller could avoid such gain if a plan of liquidation is adopted and the inventory is sold in bulk, but any LIFO reserve would be subject to a recapture tax similar to that applicable to depreciation reserves on fixed assets.

The seller would want to assign the excess value to assets in the following order:

Land.

Patents.

Buildings.

Machinery and equipment.

Inventories.

This order would minimize the seller's tax liability. The purchaser would strive to have the excess value applied in the reverse order. This should further emphasize the adversity of interest that the parties demonstrate in allocation of the purchase price.

It might appear that it would be best for the buyer and seller *not* to stipulate any allocation of proceeds, so that each could allocate the proceeds in a manner most advantageous for his purposes, and file tax returns based on this disparate treatment. Such a device is not likely to be successful. The Internal Revenue Service could put the taxpayers in a worse position than if they had stipulated an allocation of proceeds in the contract. The strong adversity of interest that each party brings to the negotiations to determine the allocation of proceeds indicates that such an allocation can rarely be upset by the Internal Revenue Service. In short, when all factors are considered, buyer and seller should agree to an allocation of proceeds as an integral part of the negotiations, even if such an agreement seems difficult to reach.

Tax-Free Reorganization.   The Internal Revenue Code at Section 368, provides for only a limited number of tax-free types of acquisition, as follows:

A   Statutory merger or consolidation
B   The acquisition of the stock of the acquired corporation in exchange for stock of the acquiring corporation
C   The acquisition of the assets of the acquired corporation in exchange for stock of the acquiring corporation

In a type A merger one or both corporations will lose their separate identities as a result of the reorganization, while in a type B reorganization the acquired corporation typically retains its legal existence as a subsidiary of the acquiring corporation.

In a tax-free reorganization no gain or loss is recognized by either party to the transaction, unless consideration other than that permitted under the code, such as cash, is received. The tax basis of the assets carries over, with no step-up permitted.

Taxable versus Tax-Free—Summary

The critical factor to be considered in determining the structure of the transaction from a tax point of view is to determine whether the tax basis of the assets is greater or less than the current exchange price. If the basis is higher than the exchange price, the buyer will prefer a tax-free reorganization so that continued tax benefits can be derived from the higher tax basis.

If the basis is lower, the buyer would prefer a taxable purchase of assets, or a purchase of stock with a subsequent liquidation, so that the tax benefits of the higher purchase price can be enjoyed.

Pooling of Interests Transactions versus Tax-Free Reorganizations

A pooling of interests is often confused with a tax-free reorganization. As indicated earlier, a pooling of interests is an accounting concept that must satisfy the requirements of APB Opinion 16, while the tax-free reorganization is a provision that must satisfy the requirements of Internal Revenue Code Section 368.

A pooling of interests is usually the desired treatment from a financial reporting perspective, while a taxable purchase is often the desired tax treatment. However, the requirements for a pooling are usually more restrictive than those for a tax-free reorganization, and a transaction that qualifies as a pooling will generally meet the requirements for a tax-free reorganization. Thus, it is very difficult, if not impossible, to achieve a taxable pooling of interests.

TAXABLE ACQUISITIONS OF STOCK—SPECIAL PROBLEMS

Sometimes the stockholders of a corporation (target) may only be interested in selling their stock in the corporation rather than the assets of the corporation. In such a situation when the purchase price of the stock is far in excess of the tax basis of the underlying assets, an acquiring corporation can still obtain the benefits of an asset purchase.

If the acquiring corporation in a taxable transaction acquires at least 80% of the target corporation stock within a 12-month period, the acquiring company can make an election to step up the basis in the underlying assets of the target corporation. In such case the cost of the stock is allocated to the various assets in proportion to their relative fair market values. However, there are certain adjustments that must be made to the tax basis of the target company's stock before the allocation. These adjustments are for unsecured liabilities assumed, earnings and profits, and for cash and cash equivalents (e.g., bank deposits, checks, etc.). For purposes of demonstrating the concept these special adjustments will be ignored in the following example.

EXAMPLE

P purchases the stock of S for $200,000 and makes an election to step up the basis of the assets. Assume that the assets of S had the following bases and fair market value:

	Basis	FMV
Inventory	$ 50,000	$ 52,500
Land	25,000	35,000
Machinery & Equipment	75,000	87,500
	$150,000	$175,000

The purchase price of $200,000 would be allocated to the assets as follows:

Inventory	($52,500/$175,000 × $200,000)	$ 60,000
Land	($35,000/$175,000 × $200,000)	40,000

Machinery & Equipment

	($87,500/$175,000 × $200,000)	100,000
		$200,000

It should be noted that the Internal Revenue Service will probably take the position that the excess of the purchase price of the stock over the fair market value of the assets should be allocated to goodwill, which is nonamortizable for tax purposes. To rebut the service's argument, the acquiring corporation could take the position, based on an independent appraisal, that if the "excess" is attributable to any intangible, it is attributable to intangibles such as patents, customer lists, and so on, that are amortizable for tax purposes. Another way to minimize an allocation of the "excess" to goodwill is to have the purchase contract specifically assign a portion of the purchase price to a covenant not to compete for a certain number of years.

Prior to The Tax Equity and Fiscal Responsibility Act of 1982 it was necessary to liquidate the acquired corporation in order to get a step-up in basis. However, now an election is made to treat the acquired corporation as if it were a new corporation that purchased the assets at the higher basis.

There are some negative aspects to obtaining a stepped-up basis for the assets of the acquired corporation. Two of the major ones are the tax costs associated with the recapture of accelerated depreciation deductions and investment tax credits. These recapture taxes could be substantial and they must be weighed against the benefit of a stepped-up basis when negotiating the purchase of stock.

TAX CONSIDERATIONS IN DETERMINING STRUCTURE FOR OPERATING BUSINESS ACQUIRED VIA PURCHASE OF ASSETS

Generally, a business that has been acquired through a purchase of assets can operate in either of the following forms:

1. Separate legal entity.
2. Division of existing corporation (acquiring corporation or subsidiary thereof).

Tax expense of the controlled group could be impacted considerably by the form in which the newly acquired business is operated, but there is no specific rule for determining which form is preferable. For each acquisition several tax considerations should be analyzed and carefully weighed along with all nontax factors in order to assure a prudent decision. These federal and state tax considerations are discussed below.

Federal Income Tax

Inventory. If election of the LIFO method is contemplated with respect to inventories of the acquired business, a significant tax benefit may be achieved in certain circumstances by combining the newly purchased assets with those of an existing corporation. The following example illustrates how inventory from an acquired business can prevent a liquidation of low-cost inventory from an existing LIFO pool.

EXAMPLE

On January 1, 1983, A Company purchases the assets of B Company, including $1,000M of inventory. A Company is a calendar-year taxpayer using the LIFO inventory method. It includes all inventories in a single pool and the composition of that pool at the beginning of 1983 is as follows:

Layer	Base Cost	Index	LIFO Cost
1976	$1,400M	1.00	$1,400M
1980	500M	1.50	750M
1982	100M	2.00	200M
	$2,000M		$2,350M

Pertinent 1983 forecast data is:

a. 12/83 Inventory @ FIFO
   A Co. product lines $2,200M
   B Co. product lines   1,100M
   Total $3,300M
b. 1983 Index A Co.   1.10
c. Cumulative Index @ 12/83
   A Co. (1.10 × 2.00)   2.20
   B Co.   1.10

The following schedules compare year-end LIFO inventories under the alternative forms of operating the business purchased from B Company:

	Layer	Base Cost	Index	LIFO Cost
a. Separate Entity				
A Co.	1976	$1,000M (1)	1.00	$1,000M
B Co.	1983	1,000M (2)	1.00	1,000M
Total		$2,000M		$2,000M
b. Div. of A Co.	1976	$1,400M	1.00	$1,400M
	1980	100M	1.50	150M
Total		$1,500M (3)		$1,550M

(1) 2200 ÷ 2.20
(2) 1100 ÷ 1.10
(3) 3300 ÷ 2.20

The $450M inventory reduction under the latter alternative translates to a $225M tax benefit. Of course, the inventories acquired from B Company must be compatible with A Company's natural business unit to achieve such a reduction, and the company would have to absorb the negative financial statement impact that the combination entails.

Start-Up Costs. The tax laws permit current deductions for certain costs only if they are paid or incurred in carrying on an active trade or business. Similar costs paid or incurred prior to commencement of business operations must be deferred and deducted over a five-year period as start-up costs. In some cases separate incorporation of purchased assets that do not yet constitute an active business enterprise could cause unnecessary deferral of tax benefits.

For example, assume that company A acquires the assets of company B, which consist entirely of a hotel and related property, and that the hotel had not begun business operations prior to the acquisition. If these assets are separately incorporated, certain preopening expenses, for example, advertising, promotion, and employee training, must be deferred. However, if company A is already in the hotel business and structures the purchased assets as a division of itself, the above expenses are currently deductible since they relate to expansion of an existing business, not start-up of a new business. Thus, when start-up costs are a factor, it may be prudent in certain cases to operate the acquired business as a division of an existing entity.

Accounting Methods. When the assets of an acquired company are structured as a division of an existing corporation, the accounting methods that have been elected by the latter generally apply to the former. Although this usually doesn't cause problems since accounting methods tend to be consistent among members of a controlled group, it could be undesirable if the existing corporation has elected to defer otherwise deductible expenses, for example, research and development expenditures, in order to enable it to utilize a loss carry-over.

State Taxes

Income Taxes. In order to understand how the form in which a newly acquired business is operated can impact total state income tax expense of a controlled group of companies, it is helpful to be familiar with the manner in which states tax multistate corporations. States are not permitted to tax companies whose in-state activities are limited to the conduct of interstate commerce, including mere solicitation of sales. Companies are required to pay tax to any state in which they exceed these activities. Income attributable to a particular state is calculated by multiplying total income by the average of three ratios or factors; that is, in-state property to total property, in-state payroll to total payroll, and in-state sales to total sales. The following example illustrates this procedure:

Company A
Computation of Georgia Income Tax
1983

Total Taxable Income		$1,000M
$\frac{\text{Instate Property}}{\text{Total Property}} = \frac{\$ 20,000M}{\$100,000M} = .20$		
$\frac{\text{Instate Payroll}}{\text{Total Payroll}} = \frac{\$ 7,500M}{\$ 50,000M} = .15$		
$\frac{\text{Instate Sales}}{\text{Total Sales}} = \frac{\$ 15,000M}{\$150,000M} = \underline{.10}$		
Total	.45	
Apportionment Factor (.45/3)		.15
State Taxable Income		150M
Tax Rate		.06
Tax		$ 9M

Analysis of this example indicates three primary methods of reducing state income taxes.

1. *Reduce Taxable Income.* If either the newly acquired business or an existing member of the acquiring company's group expects losses in the current year, state taxable income can be reduced by operating the loss company as a division of a profitable company. Since most states don't permit consolidated tax returns, losses of a separate legal entity would generally not result in any state benefit. A few states do permit operating losses to be carried back and forward.

2. *Minimize Apportionment Factors.* Most companies are not required to file tax returns in every state that imposes an income tax. Since many companies do have sales and/or payroll in states where they are not required to file returns, the aggregate of all the factors used to apportion income to states in which returns are filed is usually less than 100%. If a newly acquired business conducts taxable activities in states where the existing corporation is not required to file, or vice

versa, operating it as a division would add to the numerator of the aggregate apportionment factor amounts that could be excludable under the separate entity approach. Thus, apportionment factors can usually be minimized by separate incorporation.

3. *Reduce Tax Rate.* Although corporate tax rates can only be reduced by law, careful planning can reduce a company's effective tax rate, that is, total state income taxes divided by total income. For example, a business with relatively low profits that is heavily concentrated in a low-tax state can be combined with a business with high profits that is heavily concentrated in a high-tax state to produce significant tax savings by reducing the effective tax rate of the combined entity.

It is necessary to compare the total combined state income tax liabilities of the new and existing businesses using both the combined and separate entity approach to determine the most desirable one.

UTILIZATION OF NET OPERATING LOSS CARRY-OVERS

Federal tax laws currently permit companies that incur net operating losses to carry such losses back 3 years and forward 15 years as deductions from income of profitable years. However, these laws impose restrictions on carry-overs of companies that are parties to certain types of acquisitions in order to prevent trafficking in loss companies for the purpose of avoiding taxes. As illustrated by the following rules, the restrictions depend on the type of transaction.

Taxable Transactions

Stock Purchase. Where 50% or more of a corporation's stock is purchased during a two-year period and the corporation changes its trade or business, use of carry-overs is prohibited even though the same corporate entity is involved. A change in trade or business can occur if the acquired company changes its product line or replaces a significant number of employees. Consequently, it is desirable to enhance the profitability of companies acquired in this manner through increased volume and efficiency rather than diversification.

Asset Purchase. Net operating loss carry-overs of the acquired company are forfeited. Therefore, in order to utilize net operating loss carry-over, the acquired company's stock must be acquired in a taxable or tax-free reorganization.

Nontaxable Transactions

Statutory Merger (Type A) or Stock for Assets (Type C) Reorganization. When shareholders of the loss company receive more than 20 percent of the net fair market value of the acquiring corporation, no reduction is made to available carry-overs. However, if former shareholders of the loss company receive less than 20% of the net fair market value of the acquiring corporation, net operating loss carry-overs are reduced by 5% for every percentage point below 20%. Often this limitation can be circumvented by forming a new wholly-owned subsidiary solely for the purpose of acquiring the loss company. Since the new subsidiary's assets subsequent to the acquisition are identical to those of the acquired company previous to the transaction, the 20% test is met and no reduction in carry-overs is required. This technique is called a "triangular" merger. Unlike a taxable transaction, no continuity of business operations is required with a nontaxable transaction.

Stock for Stock (Type B) Reorganization. No reduction of net operating loss carry-overs is required.

If a consolidated tax return is filed, carry-overs originating in preacquisition years normally may be offset only against income generated by the loss company or its successor. If the loss company cannot generate sufficient income, it can be liquidated into a profitable company in an attempt to utilize the carry-overs. However, the Internal Revenue Service will probably claim that the acquisition and liquidation constitute a single transaction, that is, a merger or asset acquisition by such profitable company and thereby attempt to restrict the carry-overs.

The Tax Reform Act of 1976 made several changes to the above rules, but the effective dates of these changes have been postponed several times. The major changes scheduled to take effect on January 1, 1984 for nontaxable transactions and July 1, 1984, for taxable transactions, are summarized below:

1. Former shareholders of the loss corporation must maintain, directly or indirectly, at least a 40% interest in the loss corporation or the available net operating loss carry-overs will be reduced. This reduction will be 3½% for each percentage point below 40% but above 20%, and 1½% for each point below 20%. For example, if former shareholders retain a 10% interest in an acquired company, loss carry-overs would be reduced by 85% (3½% (40-20) + 1½% (20-10)). This change applies to both taxable and nontaxable transactions.

2. Continuity of business operations is no longer required in taxable transactions.

3. Stock for stock (Type B) reorganizations are subject to the same rules as other nontaxable transactions.
4. The tax benefits of triangular mergers are eliminated.

The Deficit Reduction Act of 1984 further delayed implementation of these changes to January 1, 1986 for both taxable and nontaxable transactions.

CONSOLIDATED TAX RETURN CONSIDERATIONS

Consolidated return implications should not be ignored when planning an acquisition. When a corporation owns at least 80% of the stock of another corporation or corporations, these corporations are eligible to file a consolidated federal tax return. Therefore, when 80% of the stock of a corporation is acquired by a corporation that is a member of a consolidated group, the acquired corporation would be considered a new member of the consolidated group. As such it must adopt the taxable year of the group, and its income will be included in the consolidated tax return of the group from the date of acquisition.

Some typical issues that must be considered prior to an acquisition involving a consolidated return situation are discussed next.

Carry-over Items

The acquiring group's utilization of the acquired company's carry-over items will be subject to separate return limitation year (SRLY) rules; that is, they can only be used against that portion of the group's consolidated taxable income that is attributable to the target corporation. This rule applies to net operating losses, capital losses, investment tax credits, and so forth.

An acquiring corporation should analyze the carry-over items to determine the acquired corporation's ability to utilize them since this could have an impact on the purchase price.

Built-in Deductions

These are deductible items such as depreciation, interest, capital losses, and so on, that are economically accrued in a preacquisition year of the acquired company but are recognized during a consolidated return year of the acquiring group. If such deductions exist, they are subject to the SRLY rules discussed above.

If doubts exist about the presence of built-in deductions, it may be advisable to insert an indemnity clause in the purchase agreement.

Thirty-Day Rule

If a corporation is acquired within 30 days of the beginning of its tax year, it can elect to be included in the consolidated return of the acquiring corporation from the beginning of its tax year.

Likewise a corporation that is acquired during the last 30 days of a consolidated group's tax year can elect not to be included in the consolidated return for that period.

Short-Period Tax Returns

In most cases it will be necessary to file a separate federal short-period return for the acquired corporation for that portion of its taxable year that preceded its acquisition by a consolidated group. Another federal return must be filed by the acquired corporation covering the period from the acquisition date to the end of the consolidated group's tax year. This return would be included in the consolidated return of the acquiring corporation.

Each period for which a return is filed is considered a tax year for purposes of utilization of carry-back or carry-over items.

Many states have similar filing requirements, but there are some states that require the acquired corporation to continue filing returns based on its original tax year unless it receives permission to change.

It should also be noted that in an acquisition qualifying as a pooling of interests for financial reporting there will be different accounting periods used for financial and tax purposes. As mentioned previously, the consolidated tax return usually will include only the income of the acquired corporation from the date of acquisition to the end of the consolidated group's tax year. However, the income of the acquired corporation will be included in the financial statements of the acquiring corporation from the beginning of the acquiring corporation's accounting period.

TAX ACCOUNTING METHODS AND PERIODS—SPECIAL CONSIDERATIONS

Tax Accounting Methods

The method of acquiring a company will generally determine the method of accounting for a specific item, such as depreciation of machinery, method of accounting for inventory, allowance for bad debts, and so forth.

Asset Acquisition. If assets of a company are purchased, the acquiring company would normally integrate the assets of the acquired company into its books and records and continue to use the same tax accounting methods it is currently using with regard to its own similar assets. However, the rules are quite complex, and accounting methods for inventory are an exception to the above rule. If the acquiring company is presently using the LIFO method, the inclusion or exclusion of the acquired company's inventory into its LIFO pool would be determined on a case-by-case basis. If the acquired and acquiring companies' inventories are homogenous, it could be included as an addition to the acquiring company's "natural business" LIFO pool. If the acquired company's inventory is not compatible or homogenous with the acquiring company's inventory, then a new LIFO election would have to be made by the acquiring company. This election could be made at the time of filing the acquiring corporation's return covering the year of acquisition. If an election is made, a separate LIFO pool would be required.

The Internal Revenue Code (Section 381) provides that a corporation that acquires the assets of another corporation in certain liquidations, mergers, and reorganizations shall carry-over the accounting methods of the acquired corporation. However, where the acquiring and acquired corporation use different methods of accounting and are operated as an integrated business unit, the predominant accounting method is used.

A company must request permission from the Commissioner of Internal Revenue Service in order to change a tax accounting method. The Internal Revenue Service has the right to challenge any tax accounting method that does not clearly reflect income.

Stock Acquisition. If stock of an acquired corporation is purchased either in a tax-free or taxable acquisition, the accounting methods that were previously used by the acquired corporation continue to be used by such corporation after the acquisition. An exception to this rule occurs if the acquired company merges into another company in a triangular reorganization. The acquired corporation would be included in the consolidated tax return of the acquiring corporation. The depreciation, inventory, and other methods of accounting continue to be used. A change in the method of tax accounting with regard to any item would have to be requested from the Commissioner of Internal Revenue Service. For example, a change may be desired for conformity where the acquired corporation was deferring research and development expenditures prior to being acquired and the acquiring corporation was currently expensing similar expenditures.

Tax Periods

The tax accounting period of the acquired corporation joining an affiliated group automatically changes to that of the acquiring corporation for federal tax purposes when a consolidated return is filed. This is not always true in the case of state tax returns.

RESEARCH TAX CREDIT

Federal tax law provides a credit equal to 25% of the excess of the taxpayer's qualified research expenditures for the current year over the average of such expenditures during a base period. Generally, the base period is the three years immediately preceding the current year.

When a company acquires all or a major portion of a business, certain adjustments are required to compute credits allowable for years ending after the acquisition. Specifically, the acquiring company must increase its base-period research costs by qualified research incurred by the acquired business during the same period.

Generally, a company is not treated as acquiring the major portion of a business merely because it acquires some assets. Instead, the transaction must include assets that the acquiring company could use to operate as a separate or distinct trade or business.

PAYROLL TAXES AND RELATED MATTERS

State Unemployment Taxes

Companies usually pay unemployment taxes to states in which they have employees at rates based primarily on their historical in-state employment experience. Those that have had few layoffs pay at relatively low rates, while those that have had severe layoffs are subject to high rates. However, the rate applicable to an acquired business can vary considerably depending on the form in which such business is operated and/or elections made by the acquiring company. Consequently, careful planning in connection with acquisitions can generate substantial tax savings.

The following discussion outlines the alternative unemployment tax rates that may apply to an acquired business and indicates the circumstances under which each rate may be available.

Preacquisition Rate of Acquired Business (Predecessor Rate). This rate will apply if the corporate structure of the acquired business is not changed. Under certain circumstances, some states also require the predecessor rate to be used by a successor corporation in other types of acquisitions, while other states merely grant the successor an option to use it.

Rate of Acquiring Company (Successor Rate). This rate will usually be required or permitted when the acquired business is operated as a division of the acquiring company.

New Employer Rate. This rate, which is normally quite high, may be required or permitted when a new corporation is formed to accommodate the acquired business. As indicated above, however, many states either permit or require such a corporation to use the predecessor rate.

Combined Rate. Certain states require or permit combinations of the predecessor's and successor's rates in connection with mergers and asset acquisitions.

In order to assure that savings are maximized with respect to unemployment taxes, it is necessary to carefully analyze the laws of each state in which the acquired company has a significant number of employees.

Social Security Taxes

If a successor–predecessor relationship is involved, any wages paid by the predecessor will be considered to have been paid by the successor for social security tax purposes. Such a relationship exists when a company acquires substantially all the property used in a business of another employer.

Targeted-Jobs Tax Credit

Employees of the acquired company can be registered with the appropriate state agency for the targeted-jobs credit by the acquiring company. Although such registration must occur prior to the acquisition date, screening and interviewing of employees to determine if they qualify for the credit can take place after the acquisition.

The maximum tax credit with respect to each eligible employee is $4500 (50% of $6000 wages in first year and 25% of $6000 wages in second year).

CHECKLIST

1. Acquiring corporation's objectives formulated.
2. Acquired corporation's objectives reviewed.
3. Form of transaction is determined:
    (a) Taxable acquisition of stock
    (b) Taxable acquisition of assets
    (c) Tax-free reorganization

4. Miscellaneous considerations:
    (a)   Utilization of carry-over items.
    (b)   Methods of accounting.
    (c)   Short tax years.
    (d)   State and federal payroll taxes.
    (e)   State income and franchise taxes.
    (f)   Consolidated tax returns

INDEX